Oberammergau Holiday

CYRIL DAVEY

Oberammergau Holiday

LONDON
EPWORTH PRESS

© *Cyril Davey 1969*

First Published in 1969
by Epworth Press

(Book Steward
Frank H. Cumbers)

Set in 12/13½pt Bembo
and printed and bound
by Billing & Sons Ltd
Guildford and London

SBN 7162 0112 7

Contents

Photographs

1) *City of the Holy Blood*

IT ALL began on Christmas Day.

One of us said: 'Where are we going next summer?' The magazines were full of 'travel-supplements', the day was crisp and cold and we thought longingly of the sunshine. I had been thinking for some time of a tour through places I had visited on other occasions – stringing together towns and countries familiar and unfamiliar to the family. We got out a large-scale map of Europe and spread it on the carpet. It took up half the floor and made our proposed journey appear formidable indeed. We folded it up and put down a small-scale one instead. That made it look more reasonable.

The holiday brochures depressed me as I flicked through the pages. One famous company had fourteen pages of Spanish beaches, twelve of Italian sands, captivating references to the sun-drenched shores of Rumania, Tunisia, Greece and Israel. What made me turn away from them was not the sameness of blue sea, crowded beaches and happily smiling visitors lying in the sun but the fact that they were all so obviously my English neighbours. We like our neighbours, fortunately. We are fond of the people we see day by day and week after week. But this idea was to . . . get away from them? No – to meet other people as well. We decided to avoid the beaches that turn you any shade from lobster-red to mahogany-brown and wander through the 'ordinary countries' somewhere between the Channel and the Mediterranean.

We mapped out an itinerary. Through the edge of Belgium into Luxembourg . . . on through Saarland and Heidelberg to the Romantic Road and Bavaria . . . past the Zugspitze into Austria. It was a hard choice between 'east through Austria and down amongst the Dolomites into Italy' or 'westwards to Switzerland'. We decided on 'west'. Vorarlberg and Liechtenstein . . . St Gallen, Lucerne and the Oberland . . . home through eastern France.

This 'first-time family car-holiday' promised a glimpse of most things Europe can offer except the sea and the beaches. Big cities and tiny hamlets; castles and cathedrals; open valleys and magnificent ranges; fairy-tale towns and a children's village. Seldom were we to be beyond the sound of running water, and seldom, as it turned out, within sight or sound of our English neighbours.

Six months later we drove hesitantly on to the S.S. *Artevelde* at Dover. We had no reason for anxiety. The Cortina served us admirably. The hotels were highly satisfactory. Language – not much English in the hotels we stayed at, but we still managed to 'get alongside people'. Time – three weeks, though we could have travelled quicker, and seen less. All in all, very successful.

Our seven countries were all very familiar, of course – the tourist lands of Europe – but for Susan and Paul they were quite new. And, mostly, to my wife too, since she had usually stayed at home in my earlier days of conducting continental holiday parties. That was a good enough reason for going.

To tell the truth, however, I had another reason. I wanted

material for a book. In 1970 the Passion Play would draw hundreds of thousands of people to Oberammergau – and not all would go as conducted parties. Besides this, though the Play is produced only once in ten years, the village is a focal-point on the itineraries of tens of thousands of tourists *every* year. Because an earlier book, *Cornish Holiday*, had drawn such appreciative letters, my publishers had suggested that 'another travel book might be a good idea'.

This is it.

It suggests, from practical experience, a slower way than some might take through Europe, and a more rewarding one – and it will serve whether it is the 'Passion Play year' or not.

The sun shone as we crossed from Dover – a contrast to a previous Ostend trip when I had been taking a conducted party to Denmark . . . and left our own tickets in the dustbin! But that is another story! Then the ship had bucked like a shying horse. Now it sailed on the sea like a duck pond at the bottom of our road in Epsom. Susan and Paul explored the ship without any inhibitions about sections which were marked 'First Class Only'. So, for that matter, did everybody else. It would have been folly to pay more than second-class fares when the freedom of the ship was yours, and not a frown on a Dutch seaman's face.

Paul came for me with a gleam in his eye. 'Got any horror comics?'

I followed him to look at the long list of prohibited imports to Belgium displayed by the purser's office. 'No dangerous drugs . . . firearms . . . parrots . . . uncooked meat . . . saccharine . . . horror comics.'

We did not even have any saccharine, and nobody asked about parrots at Ostend.

The coastal resorts of Belgium have lost the magnetism of less affluent pre-war days, when a 'continental holiday' meant ten days at Blankenberge. Ostend is no more than a staging-post and few who disembark here are likely to remember the name of the Englishman, John Kerr, who brought it sudden and brief glory.

Like most 'resorts' it began as a fishing-village. In the 13th century it struggled with the sea and the marshes, and gained the dignity of a town charter. In the 16th, it resisted the Spaniards, when its inhabitants were the only Protestants in this part of the Netherlands. One Spanish duke looked at its fortifications, and went away. A second took four years to capture it, and then deported all its Protestant inhabitants to Holland and repopulated the town with Flemish Catholics.

But it was in the beginning of the 18th century that John Kerr turned its mind from military defence to commercial attack. He founded the Ostend East India Company, and Flemish business acumen raised it to such prosperity that its fleets challenged French, Dutch and British interests in the East – until the Austrians, who then ruled Belgium, closed it down at the insistence of the 'great powers'. By 1729 its brief burst of international glory was over. While the British and French, who had together disposed of the Dutch East India Company, were left to fight things out in India, Ostend turned to oysters! They brought nearly as much profit and did nothing to provoke international complications.

Once off the boat our first anxiety was whether we would manage to drive 'on the wrong side of the road'. We slipped into it as easily as we did into the decimal system, and ended up wondering why the British must be the only Europeans out of lane.

From Ostend to Brussels the land is as flat as the Dutch polders, its colour a peaty brown. This is the beginning of the Great North European Plain. The only 'hill' between Ostend and Ghent is a gentle slope over the railway – and there is apparently only one railway tunnel between here and Moscow.

Flat though it was we found the country pleasant, with white farm-houses dotted amongst miniature copses – but the name 'Flanders' epitomises the people's struggle. A contraction of the Flemish *vlae landerren*, meaning flat land, easily flooded, it links Flemish and Dutch in the same Netherlands fight to save or reclaim their living-space.

A Belgian on the boat had asked me a question which startled me, and then gone on to expound the point of it.

'How many Belgian *au pair* girls have you known in England?'

'French, German, Austrian, Swiss, Scandinavian – yes,' I agreed. 'But no Belgians.'

'We don't emigrate, you see,' he said, 'even to learn English. Perhaps we are stuck in our own mud; perhaps it's because we won our land the hard way. We grow engineers, and we export capital . . . but not people. We built Heliopolis, and we made the Paris *Metro* . . . but our people like to stay at home. You don't find us as tourists, much. Every Belgian wants to own his farm, his own bit of land, however small it is.'

The *ghem*, *zel* and *zele* of so many Flemish place-names all mean 'house' and I thought of his words as we looked at tiny farm-houses on each side of the road. Many looked finished at one side but flat at the other, as if they had been chopped out of a terrace. Belgian law says that if you build a house against an existing house you must pay half the cost of the original party wall. The smallholder builds hopefully and waits, in vain, for a half-witted neighbour – who, instead, builds his own house, flat wall and all, a little way off . . . and waits just as hopefully for some other 'sucker'.

Tourists will always argue about 'booking ahead'. You may get held up; wish to stay longer; or want to go in the opposite direction. We booked six months ahead, saved ourselves frenzied searches, and only twice changed our minds. How? Short on money, we got the hotel lists for each area from the

national tourist offices and worked up from the lower end of
the list. Sometimes we just liked a name, or took someone's
recommendation. The *Fodor* guides, in particular, were invalu-
able, not only for 'inexpensive' and 'rock-bottom' hotels (their
phrase) but for background reading. Once, too, they just saved
me from disaster.

We had posted all our reservations, except one to Ehrwald,
and then run out of International Postal Reply coupons. On the
way to the post office for another I bought the new Fodor
Austria and skimmed through it. Would our choice be mentioned? Yes. Ehrwald . . . *Zugspitzbahn Alpenhotel* . . . 50 beds
. . . 12 baths . . . 4,040 feet. I nearly shouted out loud. It was
half-way up the Zugspitze, the highest mountain in Germany!
Three nights in Ehrwald . . . 4,000 feet down the funicular for
coffee in the village . . . 4,000 feet back for lunch!

We would certainly have remembered our holiday!

Twelve miles from Ostend a signpost beckoned us to
'Brugge'. We know it as Bruges, though we seldom remember
that Zeebrugge is really Bruges-on-Sea. The towers and spires
rose majestically ahead of us.

We drove up a narrow street and stopped in a miniature
square. Three old ladies in photogenic scarlet jumpers sat by
the doors of the little houses, making lace handkerchiefs. They
looked up briefly, hopefully, their fingers still threading intricate patterns. To make a handkerchief of this delicacy, they
told us, seldom takes less than nine hours. And they earned no
more than sixpence an hour. In the centre of the square was a
walnut tree, ancient when these old women's grandparents
were young, and beyond it a gabled building of red brick,
bronzed by the sunlight. The Rembrandt-Rubens hotel. Our
first stopping-place.

Inside, we stepped into old Flanders – as, outside, we strolled
through it. Once the home of a Flemish artist, Dobbelacre,

whose stained-glass windows are to be seen in the town hall, the house can have been little changed, downstairs, since his time. Tempted at first to relax, after our early start, we resisted the comfortable beds and set out to explore the town instead. It is surprising how much of a town can be seen in a short time with the help of a town-plan, sought from the tourist office and studied before you leave home. To breathe its atmosphere is another matter. You must avoid the same-as-everywhere hotels – and talk to all the citizens you can. Even shopkeepers.

With Ypres and Ghent, Bruges completes a trio of art-treasures in stone, brick, cobbles and paint that is hard to match anywhere outside Italy. After even a day in Bruges you will travel with a richer mind and a lighter heart for the rest of your journey. It is so full of treasures that I cannot mention a hundredth of them. It is one of the truly individual towns of Europe.

The strange thing is that this *ville morte*, the 'dead town' of Flanders, was once throbbing with life. Its green canals, sluggishly lapping the grey stone walls, are all that is left of a rich seaport. 'Brugge' was the 'bridge' on the river Zwin which made this little city as opulent as any in Europe when Brussels was no more than a staging-post. When Canute's queen, Emma, took refuge here from her bastard son, Harold, she found it already full of merchants. By the 12th century wool was imported from England to meet the demands of the weavers. A hundred years later seventeen countries had trading representatives here, and Bruges woollen goods were on sale from France to Muscovy, from the Baltic to the Mediterranean. In its shops were Italian silks, Russian furs and Arabian spices. The harbour clattered with tall-masted ships. Then, slowly but relentlessly, came disaster, dropped by the waters of the river Zwin that had once brought prosperity. Drifting in with the sea-tide, sand fell to the bottom of the river until, like Tregony in Cornwall, all that remained was a stream running sluggishly over the silt. By the end of the 14th century the great days of the city should have been over.

They would have been, but for the luxurious court of Burgundy.

The splendour-loving Dukes of Burgundy (Philip the Bold the most colourful of them all) established their court here in the 15th century. John Paston, in his *Letters*, claimed that there was 'no other court like the Burgundians except that of King Arthur' – the exotic Arthur of Mallory. For a hundred years it was crowded not only with soldiers and hangers-on, but with poets, chroniclers, artists and craftsmen. Amongst them were the painters van Eyck and Hans Memling.

This great glory shone for a hundred years after the Zwin had dwindled to a stream. By then the Burgundians, too, had had their day and Bruges died until 19th-century travellers, searching for 'romance', discovered the city once more. That it remains unspoiled by its new prosperity is largely due to its wise burghers, who insisted that all new building must match the character of the old.

There are three special treasures in Bruges and the first we sought out as we began our late afternoon's exploration. It is in the church of *Onze Lieve Vrou* (Our Lady) which contains the mausoleum of Mary of Burgundy and her father, Charles the Rash. The church's real glory, however, is the little white marble Madonna and Child by Michelangelo. Placed well above eye-level, the Madonna, charming undoubtedly, seemed to look down on us with a slightly disdainful smile.

We walked by what remained of the prosperous river, its modern trade now only motorboats full of tourists, and into the Grote Markt where the country folk were packing away the last of their unsold flowers, butter and vegetables. Two features of the square are characteristic of all these Flemish towns: the Belfry and the Cloth Hall. The Hall, brick-built, has pride of place, taking up almost one whole side of the square. Here the woollen cloth which made Flanders prosperous was sold, and the need for a long, clear space determined its size and shape. On the opposite side of the square are the gabled houses of the burghers and the guilds, and above them rises the Belfry and Halles with the famous carillon which chimes every quarter-hour. Where the stalls were now being packed away the weavers, under their leader Jakob van Artevelde, had long ago fought bloody battles with their patrician masters, forming themselves into a mediaeval trade union as anathematised by their masters as were their 19th-century counterparts. But violence, now, seems a long way off in lovely Bruges.

There were days, later in our journey, when it required an effort for some of us to go and 'see the sights', but tonight nothing could keep us in. Our meal was simple, and memorable only for the elderly lady whose daughter was trying to keep her in the narrow way.

'I'm in a foreign country, dear, and I don't see why I should drink water when there are all these other interesting-looking things!'

The friendly *hotelier* was emphatic as we went out. 'You *must* go on the canals and see the illuminations. Our city is lovely by day . . . but by night it is exquisite.'

He was quite right. All mediaeval towns change character as the sun sets. They slip back by centuries as the hours advance, until in the after-midnight silence the modern world is gone. The Bruges canals weave in and out of the old buildings and our guide did not talk too much. The lights played on the ancient stones. We drifted below the bridge guarded by St Johannes Nepomuk, the patron saint of all bridges, whom we were to find again in Heidelberg. Beside it was the grey, grave house where the Spanish merchant, Perez de Maluenda, once hid the sacred relic of the Holy Blood. Farther along the Dijver stood a white house. 'They filmed part of *The Nun's Story* there,' said the guide. Farther still, the Brangwyn museum. 'In

B

Britain they think Frank Brangwyn was English because he painted murals in the House of Commons. But no, he is Flemish . . . a great artist from a land of artists.'

Above us, in the belfry, the *carillon* chimed its nightly hour-long concert, the bells surging and diminishing as we chugged slowly through the mazy waterway. We made out some Schubert . . . 'The British Grenadiers' . . . a tinkle of Chopin . . . 'Mine eyes have seen the glory . . .' The men of Bruges have a catholic, if simple taste, or else they strive to please all comers.

When we walked home the streets were empty and our own little square more silent still. We had dawdled slowly enough to look in the shops, finding life and death displayed proudly side by side. The florists' displays were sumptuous – but not more so than the coffin-shops'. People in Flanders must save up all their life for death. The coffins were immense, frighteningly solid, ornamented with silver plates, or topped with brass rails and brass knobs. The price, tempting the most avid for life, ranged round £50 and upwards. The 'dead city' looked an expensive place to die in.

To stay and see; or to go on and see something else – that is the ultimate dilemma of touring, and the room booked at the next stop is sometimes the anchor one needs in the future. There were far too many things I wanted to see in Bruges and one of them I really regretted missing – the house of the Guild of the Archers of Saint Sebastian. The Guild is as ancient as the Crusades, and membership of it highly prized. Our own Charles II was a member when he was in exile. The first Guards Regiment was founded in Bruges at that time and its present Colonel-in-Chief, Queen Elizabeth II, is an honorary member of the Guild. Shooting takes place three evenings a week – though the public is only admitted during the day-time – at a target very different from the normal circles of the archery clubs. A shuttlecock is placed on a *perche*, by tradition twelve feet higher than any other in Belgium.

The second treasure of Bruges I found by going along the lovely canal by the Quai de Rosaire, turning through the fish-market, up the Street of the Blind Ass (such enchanting names these towns retain!) and into the Place du Bourg. Here stands the oldest Town Hall in the Netherlands, begun in 1376, with statues and bas-reliefs along its frontage; the 18th-century Palace of Justice; and the renaissance Recorder's House with a gilded façade. The building I sought is crowded into a corner of the square. More truly it is two chapels, the crypt dating back to the 11th century, and the upper chapel built three hundred years later. There, in a superb golden reliquary, is the most venerated treasure of all Belgium, for this is the Chapel of the Holy Blood. In the 12th century, say the chroniclers, the Patriarch of Jerusalem gave to Thierry d'Alsace a precious relic in recognition of his bravery in the Second Crusade – a drop of Christ's blood shed on the cross. In an age of credulity the Count brought back the holy relic to the city of Bruges. To guard it the Confrerie du Saint Sang was founded, with members from thirty patrician families of the district. Their descendants still take their duties with utmost seriousness and, before the relic is exposed each Friday, they attend mass in the chapel.

Modern piety is equally devout in Catholic Belgium, as the annual procession demonstrates. Each May the *ville morte* is crowded, vibrant with spiritual zeal. The Procession of the Holy Blood travels many miles, and contains tableaux from the Bible and the mythology of the Church. But its centre is the great reliquary of the Holy Blood. Sightseers with their cameras and flash-bulbs are an incongruous intrusion. To the thousands of pilgrims from all over Belgium this first Monday after the 2nd May is a religious occasion as significant as the Passion Play is to the villagers of Oberammergau.

Belgium is a great country for 'folklore', an umbrella-word
covering museums, costumes, furniture, horn-blowing, processions, flag-throwing and a great deal else. What began as
local custom has been turned to advantage by the tourist
industry. There are three thousand annual processions in
Belgium – religious, like the Holy Blood, in Flanders; secular
in Wallonia. There are inter-town competitions, which
naturally include flag-throwing and, more unexpectedly, eating contests. The stupendous beer-drinking bouts of the
Bavarian carnivals are matched here by the 'eating fêtes' when
the object is to see who can devour the largest quantity of
heavy, puddingy food before the bell rings. Most of the 'folklore' is truly ancient, as in Ypres, for instance, where cats are
flung from the church tower. Modern sentiment insists on
stuffed ones, though once they were real enough. But be a little
cautious of some of the claims of antiquity. At least one brilliant
publicity-minded folklorist has himself invented for the tourist
trade a few 'colourful ceremonies whose origins are lost in the
mists of time'.

The third of the Bruges treasures was only a few hundred
yards from the narrow lane that led to our hotel. Painting, in
Flanders, developed from the schools of the illuminators. Its
content was pious, its style realistic and down-to-earth. One of
the early masters, Hans Memling (1430?–95) ranked in his time
only second to the van Eycks. His religious paintings are restrained and deeply beautiful, his portraits dignified and
strangely alive. The Memling collection is housed not in an art
gallery but in the Hospital of St John. I entered through a deep
archway, expecting to find a quiet courtyard with geraniums
lining closed windows. After all, the 'hospital' was founded in
1188. Instead, there was a porter at the gate, a bustle of out-
patients and a sharp smell of antiseptic, for the ancient hospital
has been in continuous use ever since its foundation. The
Memling collection is displayed in a spacious and lofty hall in

this busy, tranquil house of healing. It is a treasure not to be missed, both for its own sake and its surroundings.

'Have you seen the dispensary?'

The question was from a grave-eyed young sister, who paused to point down a passage-way. I have no great affection for dispensaries, but as soon as I pushed open the door I saw why she had sent me. I was back in the time of Hans Memling himself. The large, rectangular room, the pharmacy of the old Hospital of St John, has shelves crowded with mediaeval jars and tuns. Pestles and mortars seemingly as old as the panelling itself stood on the benches. Yet this is no place of relics. Dispensers were still making up prescriptions in what is probably the oldest working dispensary in the world.

The lace-makers by the cream-washed walls were still busy as we loaded the car. Before we left we walked along the lane to the *beguinage*, where swans circled graciously by the bridge over the canal. Peculiar to Belgium, the *beguines* were an order of secular nuns who wore white caps and black robes, took no vows, but lived communally by the rules of their Order, usually in little cottages set terrace-wise round an open green. Though the Order was dissolved in 1928, some of them still exist. To pass through the gate of the *beguinage* was to move into a world of peace and utter tranquility. Thin-stemmed trees shaded the green square, and here and there a black-robed figure flitted amongst the low cottages. We left quietly, feeling we had been where the outside world had no real place.

Not far along the canal is the quietest stretch of canal in Bruges, endlessly photographed, its placidity disturbed only by the swans. This is the Minnewater – the Lake of Love. Make what entrancing legends you will out of the name. In fact, it is all that remains of the inner harbour of Bruges from the years of its splendour.

Chastened by the beauty of the past we walked back to the little square to begin our second day's journey. Peace was

shattered as a van jolted past us, its driver stopping to ring a
clashing handbell by the walnut tree. Immediately half a dozen
women, with a couple of boys and some neat girls, surged out
of the houses. All of them carried jugs, basins or saucepans.
They clustered about the van like English children round an
ice-cream cart. But it was not ice-cream. In a dozen huge con-
tainers in the open van was soup – pea soup, asparagus soup,
celery soup, vegetable soup, any kind of soup you might be
likely to want. All you had to do was keep it warm. The smell
of it drifted across the cobbles and the women were still clack-
ing cheerfully as we drove off. We did not see whether anyone
from the Rembrandt-Rubens hotel had come out to replenish
their stock.

2) *Everything Closes at Twelve*

'YOU *must* see the orchids in Ghent!'

The instruction was from a friend who is a devoted grower.

'You *must* see the four "musts" of Ghent,' proclaimed the town's publicists. They included the abbey, the tryptich and a museum but did not mention the orchids.

I know of no town whose publicity literature is more inviting or more opulent. Indeed, were it not for the lush hand-outs from Bavaria . . . from Austria (slightly less affluent) . . . from Switzerland (a brochure for every village, and all with a chair-lift) . . . from France (almost all in French) . . . we might have been tempted to spend our whole holiday in Belgium. But, because we had stayed so long in Bruges and planned to be over the Luxembourg frontier by evening, we had only a couple of hours for the second of Flanders's art-towns.

There was one thing, however, that Paul specially wanted to see: Jan van Eyck's tryptich of the 'Adoration of the Golden Lamb'.

From Bruges to Brussels the road is flat, featureless and speedy and the motorist may easily take no notice at all of the 'Ghent' sign. This is a pity, for the town has a great deal to offer. Even so, after Bruges, it is an anticlimax – just as we found later on the Romantic Road, where the loveliness of Dinkelsbuhl was spoiled by the opera-set charms of Rothenberg. The reason is clear. Bruges clings to its past. Ghent, on the other hand, is a city with a firm place in the 20th century. It is a city very much alive, in contrast to the *ville morte*. The contrast is due to the fact that the river silted up in Bruges while it continued to flow swiftly at Ghent, where the wharves are still full and busy. Its streets are crowded, its shops full and its population a quarter of a million.

To mention 'the river' is less than just. Ghent has three rivers, the Lys, the Live and the Scheldt. Indeed, it is built on a hundred or more islands. As a textile centre it is the Manchester of the Netherlands. Its horticultural trade is probably the foremost in Europe. And the seaport at the northern end of the city was of great strategic importance when Belgium, in 1944, became a key-point in the Rhine armies' supply-line. The holiday travel-ler, who is usually content to leave his own world behind and take other people's prosperity for granted, may recall that not a little of modern Ghent's prosperity was due to the shrewdness of a certain Ghent burgher who smuggled one of Britain's inventions out of England.

Lieven Bauwens, for his part, might have claimed that he was only getting his own back, since it was England which ruined the wool-weavers of Flanders.

The story begins a long time ago.

Belgium's historical complexities are too many to be followed with ease, and it is enough to say that when they were not fighting against the Great Powers the Belgians were often struggling amongst themselves. In Flanders this conflict was frequently between the towns' overlords and the weavers who were the basis of their prosperity. The 'finest hours' for the common people of Belgium were when they massacred the

French at the 'Matines of Bruges', led by the master-weaver, Pieter de Conineck, and again when they defeated the French chivalry in the Battle of the Golden Spurs, in 1302. Their triumph did not last long. French dictatorship was reasserted and the only effective resistance continued in Bruges.

We did not get into the Castle of the Counts of Flanders. It was closed when we arrived. But nothing inside could have been more impressive than the exterior, unless it might be its exhibition of mediaeval instruments of torture. The castle is built a little outside the hub of the old town, a slightly contemptuous gesture signifying that the Counts ruled Ghent but were not particularly interested in its welfare. There was a time, not long after the Battle of the Golden Spurs, when a greater interest might have altered the history of Europe. The Counts maintained a tenuous alliance with the ruling power, France. England, on the other hand, opposed French interests and was concerned to build up its own economy. One means of doing both was to cut off the supply of English wool – the best in Europe – from the Flemish weavers, and so prevent their competition. The Flemings began to feel the pinch. Then the weavers' leader, Jakob van Artevelde, made up his mind to a dangerous piece of expediency. Challenging the authority of the Counts of Flanders, in order to save the commoners from starvation and regain imports of wool, he made a secret alliance with Edward III of England and agreed to recognise his claim to the French throne. Nothing could better illustrate the power of the weavers of Flanders.

Ghent's *Vrijdagmarkt* – the Friday Market – was throughout the middle ages the scene of political activity and bloody strife. As we looked at the statue of van Artevelde in his mediaeval tribune's robes, we remembered that we had come to Belgium on the ferry-boat that bore his name. Here in this square was detonated the war which ensured the place in history of a dozen French and English kings, for it was where his statue now stands

that the master-weaver, one snowy day in January 1340, proclaimed Edward III to be King of France. With that proclama-
tion began the Hundred Years War. It made or ruined kingly
reputations and wrote large the names of small towns into
history . . . Crécy, Poitiers, Agincourt . . . the Black Prince,
Henry V . . . even Sir John Falstaff. To Ghent it meant one
thing in particular – the renewed and prosperous association of
the Flemish weavers with the sheep and the merchants of
England.

All that may seem a long way from a piece of commercial
chicanery at the beginning of the last century. By then Ghent
had almost forgotten the splendid days of her brave weavers.
Indeed, by the time the Industrial Revolution had blackened the
skies of 18th-century England the city had turned first to the
grain trade and then to the linen industry. It was in 1800 that
history twisted once more. A leading Ghent citizen, Lieven
Bauwens, was visiting England where, in mills and mines,
toiled the unwanted children of the poor. One of the leading
industrialists was Sir Richard Arkwright, whose home on the
banks of the Derwent, Willersley Castle, is now a popular
Methodist holiday home. It was he who invented one of the
first effective power-looms, the 'Spinning Jenny'. The man
from Ghent saw it when he visited Arkwright's mills.

There were no customs formalities in those days. Bauwens
returned home with Arkwright's secret in his mind. Following
him that same year, piece by piece in the baggage of trusted
friends, came the 'Spinning Jenny'. Patterned on Arkwright's
invention, the weaving machines were made by the score. A
new prosperity swept over Ghent. In ten years the cotton
industry exploded. There were weaving factories employing
10,000 people, many of them housed outside the city in
emergency camps.

Ghent's famous museums have pottery, pictures and 'folklore' to fascinate the visitor. But they have something else, too.

The 'Spinning Jenny' stands in the Folklore Museum for all to
see . . . a tribute to Belgian craft rather than Belgian art. But it
is not surprising that Burgomaster Bauwen's statue stands not
far from that of the tribune van Artevelde, just outside the
castle of Gerard the Devil, which looks out over the river,
silent and forbidding.

We never found out why Gerard should have been regarded
as a devil.

Nor did we get into his castle.

We were making (as I said before I began meandering
through Ghent history) for the first two 'musts' of the city, the
cathedral of St Bavon and the triptych. St Bavon was a
lecherous nobleman converted late in life, who scarcely deserved
his halo. Outside, the massive cathedral lacks the grace or
secular splendour of much Flemish architecture, but we were
prepared to be more impressed by what it contained. Jan van
Eyck, Memling's contemporary at the Burgundian court, has
left to us in this church one of the priceless masterpieces of all
time. It is a detailed painting, in three sections, which is not
only almost unbelievably brilliant in colour and almost
inexhaustible in content, but is one of the earliest known paintings in oil. That it has survived at all is something of a miracle.
The nude figures of Adam and Eve were clothed in new paints
by order of a prudish emperor. The central panel was filched
for the Louvre, and only returned from Paris after the fall of
Napoleon. The triptych was stolen by the Germans in the First
World War and again, by Goering's order, in the Second. Like
the Chalice of the Holy Blood, it was only recovered some
years after the war ended – in this case, from an Austrian salt
mine near Salzburg.

We tried the cathedral's main door. It was shut. We went
round to the side door. That was shut firmly, too. So was the
third. Then I looked at my watch.

Did I say we did not get into the castle of the Counts? Nor

into the Castle of Gerard the Devil? We did not get into the
Belfry or the Halles, either. Nor the Mansion of the Rear
Sickle nor the House of the Small Sickle.

Our watches pointed to 12.30.

And I should have remembered.

Continental Europe has an unbreakable habit of midday
somnolence. Churches, abbeys, museums, castles, belfrys, even
the bigger shops and a lot of the smaller ones observe it. At two
o'clock you are safe once more.

But everything closes at twelve.

Except the cafés, fortunately. After coffee and a cake we
looked at *Dulle Griet*, the iron cannon bearing the arms of
Burgundy, cast in van Artevelde's day and whose name in
English is 'Mad Meg'. It did not really make up for van Eyck.
We did not even try to find the other 'must' – the ruins of the
Abbey, where Edward III's son was born. His name was John
of Gaunt, a famous name in the chronicles, but it was only here
that I realised it was an anglicised form of 'John of Ghent' and
not a description of the cadaverous figure I had always sub-
consciously imagined.

One thing the clocks of Ghent could not rob us of – the
view from St Michael's bridge. They say it is at its best in the
evening sunlight, and I can well believe it, but even at midday
the vista was superb. The castle lay in the background. The
spires of the town rose into the blue sky, clear amongst them
that of St Bavon – against which I still felt a private grudge.
The pinnacle of the belfry is topped by a gilded dragon which,
tradition has it, was brought back by a Crusader from Istanbul.
But the loveliest of all sights from here are the splendid Guild
Houses on the Graslei, the old *quai des herbes*. They were the
most exquisite buildings we found in Ghent. Steep-roofed,
with the sharp angle softened by the stepped stonework, their
frontages carved without over-elaboration and lightened with
rectangular windows, they date from five centuries, beginning

with the 13th. Even their names stir the imagination . . . the House of the Corporation of Free Boatmen . . . the Tollhouse . . . the Grain Measurer's House . . . the House of the Corporation of Masons . . . the Spijker. The masons built them to last for ever, for they could never imagine a day when their city would not be in the eyes of the world.

Reluctantly, we turned our back on them, bought crisp rolls in a little bakery whose owner could not have known that twelve o'clock had struck, and set off towards Brussels.

Brussels was not our goal, for we had much farther to go, and we wondered how we were going to navigate our first big town. We need not have worried. Brussels caters admirably for those who do not wish to stay, and gets rid of them as soon as it can, by fast lanes and through tunnels until, before you have time to get lost, you are out on the other side of the town sweeping through green parkland towards the forest.

Nevertheless, I felt chagrined by our haste, for Brussels is, without doubt, one of the loveliest cities in northern Europe. Even so, though many travellers will press on from the coast in order to spend the rest of the day here, I would still commend the quietness of Bruges to those who want to adjust to a mood of holiday forgetfulness.

A better plan, if you can, is to stop in Brussels on the way home. The 'classy' shops are exclusively expensive, but the departmental stores are cheap, and have the most inexpensive restaurants in the city. Not that you need to eat inexpensively. In a city where eating rates high among the pleasures, restaurants range from tiny ones catering for the gourmets and the élite to those which specialise in Congo food for Belgian ex-colonials.

As a rule the tourist – if he is like us – saves his money and goes sight-seeing and shop-gazing. And from the boulevard to the flea-market there is plenty to be seen. Indeed, had we spent a couple of hours there instead of Ghent it would have been

hard to decide what to go and see. The Grand' Place, of course
– even more flamboyant under its nocturnal illumination . . .
the Petit Sablon, the square with forty-eight small statues each
representing some 16th-century Bruxellois trade . . . the house
of the reformer Erasmus . . . the house where Wellington
danced at the Duchess of Richmond's ball on the eve of
Waterloo . . . the Opera House, the Theatre de la Monnaie,
where an operatic aria sparked off the revolution which gained
Belgian independence after a score of centuries of foreign
rule.

Inevitably, I suppose, we would have gone to see the
Minnikin-pis. The fascination of this tiny boy, acting as a fountain by performing the most natural function in the world, is
astounding. He has been there, this little bronze boy, since the
17th century, and even then he only replaced a stone predecessor who threatened to crumble away. Why he should be there
at all nobody knows. The legends about him are lewd or sentimental, according to the teller's taste. Amongst the first kind is
the assertion that this little burgomaster's son (for they agree,
at least, in that) persistently 'sprayed' a Spanish sentry under the
house in the days of Spain's rule over Belgium. The sentimental insist that the boy got lost and his father promised to
give the city a statue representing him just as he was found.
But these tales take no account of the fact that the great
Burgundian, Philip the Good, had a similar little boy, similarly
occupied, though with rose-water, to garnish a cake at one of
his most magnificent banquets. However primly the prudes
may look, the *Mannikin* is the pride of Brussels. Its 'oldest
citizen', he has a wardrobe full of uniforms, from those of the
French Revolution to a modern Boy Scout's – though none.
be it said, are Spanish.

Yet perhaps the one thing I would like to have looked up in
Brussels was the telephone book. It is the exemplification of
democracy. Between the Palais du Pneu and the Palais de Sport

is the entry 'Palais du Roi'. Yet perhaps, even so, the king might not answer the phone.

As we tunnelled under the busy traffic there was time for none of these things, after all. We sought them out on another holiday. We went out like heroes under the triumphal gates, slowly through the park and the forest and on to the motor-way. Esch-sur-Sure was still more than a hundred miles away – and it was gone half-past four. We were still waiting for our picnic tea.

3) *The Saracen's Head*

THE QUICKEST way from Brussels to Luxembourg is probably through Bastogne to Arlon, with a proper frontier-post where guards and policemen will salute you. We, on the other hand, were entering Luxembourg through the back-door, or at least by a side entrance – and as I was eating my late picnic tea I remembered a courier who once assured her party, in a dull moment, that she had to go all the way back to Italy to get her passport stamped. It was not done when she came in, she insisted, and she could not now get out of France until she could prove she had got in. There *are* countries like that, of course, and though I suspected the story it came into my mind when I re-read some 'Hints to Drivers on the Continent'. *Always get your passport stamped*, it said, *especially if you have a car.*

The only reason we were not going the more direct way was so that we could spend a night at Esch-sur-Sure – and that, just because I had been fascinated by a photograph of the village, looking remote, romantic and slightly bizarre. Esch, however, was still a long way off when we packed the *gaz* stove into

Bruges: the belfry

Esch-sur-Sure, Luxembourg

St John Nepomuk, Patron Saint of Bridges

the boot of the Cortina and took the road to Namur – described
in the itinerary as 'moderately fast and of no particular scenic
interest'. In fact, it is excessively dull – with delectable countryside on the edge of it. One can tear on to Namur almost without realising that the lovely Meuse valley crosses the road at
right-angles. True, the river-road is better suited to carts than
cars; and time, now, was our adversary. The only thing would
be to come back to Belgium another day.

But even if you have no time for the Meuse valley you must
pause in Namur.

The houses are tidy and neat, with a pinkish air about them.
The citadel stands above the town and here the modest river
Sambre meets the history-laden Meuse. There seems little to
write home about, no reason even for a picture postcard. Yet
like the countryside itself, the two treasures of Namur are
hidden from the traveller who only stops for coffee and the
toilets.

In the Convent of the Sisters of Notre Dame is to be seen the
finest work of Hugo d'Oignies, the master jeweller and silver-
smith. The inventive and naturalistic decoration is that of an
artist who had an eye for the detail of his native countryside.
Squirrels, horses, stags, harts one might have expected. The
more bizarre *motif* in these sacred bowls and crosses is the men
on stilts. In this silver ornamentation they have a grotesque
quality which could only be matched by the strange stork-like
silhouettes of men on real stilts against the Walloon twilight.

Why did the men of this region use stilts at all? Obviously
because when the Meuse overflows its banks they kept people's
feet dry in days before rubber thigh-boots were invented. This,
of course, is too simple for the folk-tale tellers. Jehan of Namur,
they say, had a rebellion on his hands and, for once in Belgian
history, the big man won. His subjects, coming to ask forgive-
ness, were repulsed by his steward with the throw-away comment that the Duke would pardon no one, whether they came

C

to plead for mercy on foot, horse, carriage or boat. The device is obvious. They came on stilts. And, naturally, the Duke was so taken with their ingenuity that he pardoned their insurrection on the spot. We might think the tale an invention of someone who invents folklore for a Tourist Office except that it occurs in an ancient chronicle.

The second of Namur's relics is far more strange and terrible. It is the heart of Don Juan of Austria who was murdered while he beseiged Namur in 1578. Illegitimate half-brother of Philip II of Spain, it was Don Juan who had beaten the Turks in the sea-battle of Lepanto and thus helped to turn back the Muslims at a moment when they threatened the security of European Christendom once more. This decisive act did not weigh with the Belgians when he pitched camp outside the walls of Namur. An 'admirer' sent him a poisoned pair of gloves from which he died. It is, in fact, no less credible than the bombs in brown-paper parcels with which modern diplomats have been killed. Though Philip, with no love for his half-brother, had 'promoted' him to the nastiest task in Europe, the governor-generalship of the Netherlands, he did at least agree that his body should be buried in Spain.

To take a royal body across Europe in those days was a costly business. Soldiers, a guard of honour, special rooms in each town they came to . . . all this cost more money than Philip would advance or Don Juan's friends possessed. Instead, they went about the business the cheap way. There would be no 'royal progress'. Cutting the Spaniard's body into pieces they wrapped them up, packed them in their saddlebags, rode across France as quickly as possible and finally reached the Spanish capital. There they sewed the broken body together, dressed it in a sumptuous court robe and presented it to the king.

Only the Duke's heart was left behind, to be buried in the cathedral of captured Namur.

I have mentioned the Walloon country, which reaches

through the Ardennes to the borders of Luxembourg. It is divided in mind and spirit from Flanders, where we had spent the previous day, and there are still Wallonians who would prefer your room to your money if you were a Flamand seeking accommodation at a remote inn. The division is as sharp as that between Welsh and English, as deep as between Eire and Ulster. The Wallonians are reminiscent of the Liverpool lady I once met. After moving south, she had returned home for a holiday. When I asked if she liked Surrey her reply was a brief: 'No!' I asked her why. Her answer was Merseyside unashamed.

'They go shopping in gluvs!'

The Wallonians probably think the Bruxellois all wear gloves, too. Certainly their scorn of those beyond sight of the Ardennes has the same note of raw superiority.

Thirty miles beyond Namur lies the dull town of Marche, its only distinction for us that it had no toilets. Not even the café had any – it was the only reason we stopped – and the proprietor merely waved his hand up a narrow street of small houses which had naught for our comfort when we trudged through it.

Amongst all the continental summer activities there are few more popular than road-mending. Between Brussels and Namur there were innumerable road-works. Between Namur and Marche they were remaking it. Beyond Marche they were tearing up half-mile stretches, so that every vehicle raised a cloud of beige dust. Our earlier mood of euphoria was rapidly ebbing away. Then, with Marche behind us, we began to see the long rolling acres of the Ardennes through the yellow mist. Although it was not yet dusk the sun was dropping and the green of the woods and forests had already taken on deeper shades. The road-makers were still at work though sensible workmen had long since resorted to the nearest bar. We might be thrusting through this sand-cloud for miles.

It was then that I saw a signpost to the left which said *Route Touristique: Ardennes.*

'Turn left!' I ordered sharply, like a map-reader on the Monte Carlo rally.

The 'Monte' navigators have usually been over the route before. We were not so lucky. We certainly dodged the road-menders on the 'A' road but not until we had gone four or five miles was it evident that we were not on a 'B', or even a 'C' or 'D' road. By that time the lanes were too narrow to turn back. We could have done with a bit of road-making on the tracks we were following. In the distance the wooded hills of the Ardennes grew nearer – and darker. No ramps on the main road could have been more painful than the ruts into which we bumped; no dust thicker than that which we left behind us – only we were going so slowly that it was not all left behind. It rose from the front wheels and came in through the back windows. It may have been *touristique* but it was hardly *scenique* . . . the views were of small shacks, a few cows and distant farm-houses with unfriendly barking dogs. Inside the car it was difficult to see the words on the A.A. route. Not that it would have helped. We were in country that A.A. route-makers had never thought of traversing. We eventually crawled down a pot-holed lane on to the main road at a hazardous point between a tiny shop and a cow-shed.

We asked a small boy the way to Bastogne and he pointed to the right. I thought we should have turned left – but I was in no position to argue. It was I who had chosen the *route touristique*! Two miles deeper amongst the woods we had to come back.

Bastogne – when we reached it – was sleepy and the 'tween-light so dim that the only photo I tried to take was a failure. It was of the American war memorial.

This, of course, is very much American country, and Bastogne itself proudly remembers its nickname of *La Nuts Cité.*

In December 1944, came the last Nazi attempt to block the allied advance on Germany, the famous 'von Rundstedt offensive'. Von Rundstedt planned a three-pronged attack towards Liège in the north, Sedan in the south and Bastogne in the centre. St Vith, the primary objective in the Liège attack, resisted. The Sedan attack was a failure. Bastogne, ill-defended, both because it was necessary to maintain armour and artillery elsewhere and because it was considered too heavily wooded for an effective German offensive, was attacked in force by Nazi tanks and armoured vehicles which came rolling out of the Ardennes. The American 106th Division were un-seasoned troops, and snow and ice turned difficult conditions into chaos. Fog hid both enemy and allies. A snowstorm, mocking the carols being sung in Germany and America, blew up as Christmas drew near. From the German commander came an order to surrender.

'Nuts!'

General Anthony McAuliffe's brisk reply passed into American war-history, and into the folklore of the town. The American memorial reminds one of it and, whereas most towns pride themselves on museums of good or indifferent art, Bastogne is most proud of its 'Nuts Museum', with relics of those terrible Christmas days in 1944 before the encircled town was eventually relieved by 2,000 American planes.

I asked if anyone wanted to try to find the 'Nuts Museum', and got three answers.

'At this time of night?'

'I'd rather have some supper.'

And, more crisply, 'Nuts!'

Esch-sur-Sure is no more than twelve miles from Bastogne, and we began to look for the frontier-post. Then, almost abruptly, it was in front of us. A notice said: '*Douane* . . . Customs . . . Luxembourg.' We stopped and waited, a Belgian flag just behind us. Ahead, a Luxembourg flag drifted in the

breeze. But that was all. No barrier. No policeman. No soldiers
with pistol-heavy holsters. We pressed the hooter of the car
but nothing happened.

'Should we go on?'

I recalled the incredible story of the courier who had to go
back from Dover to Italy to get her passport stamped. It was
all nonsense – but the *Hints to Drivers* had insisted. '*Always get
your passport stamped.*'

We put our hand on the horn and kept it there. Not even a
cow responded. The little whitewashed cottage by the roadside, its television aerial thrusting smugly upwards, seemed
uninhabited. I went up to the door and knocked. Nobody
answered, and I went round the back. A man was digging at
the top of the garden, his shirt half in, half out of his blue
trousers, a basket of potatoes by his side.

'Uh?' His grunt and tilted head were a universal language.
'At this time of night . . .? Or 'What the hell . . .?'

I waved my passports at him, all four of them.

He shrugged and picked up his spade. When he had drawn
another root of potatoes he looked up again, apparently surprised to see me still there.

'*Va t'en!*' That was all. 'On your way, mate!'

'No stamp?' they asked, as I got into the driving seat.

'It's this Common Market,' I explained. 'Belgium and
Luxembourg, you know.' But it could hardly have been
merely the Common Market. Only once or twice amongst a
score of customs-houses did anyone ask to see a passport. Not
once did anyone stamp them. Taking a car round Europe is
easier than most people imagine.

The surprising thing about frontiers is that, for the most part,
the country seems much the same on the other side. The only
difference here was that the Ardennes woodlands began darkly
to hem us in. There was no other traffic and, indeed, no pedes-
trians on this quiet road. Within a mile or so, we came to a

little signpost which directed us alongside the Sure. We were tired, hungry, grubby, grimy and uneasy. It was gone nine o'clock, and continental hotels tell you that they will not reserve your room after 6 p.m. unless you phone.

The river was running black under the night-sky. We passed through a tunnel, turned left and through a second tunnel, drove a couple of hundred yards – and found ourselves back where we had started. We had driven right round Esch-sur-Sure! Half way round again and two minutes later, opposite a trim stone bridge across the river, we found the pink-washed Hotel du Nord. M. Neckar-Ney greeted us warmly in French, called his son who enquired after our health and our journey in very good English, and started unloading the car almost before we were out of it. The locals in the bar stared frankly and nodded, while Madame apologised that the dinner was finished an hour before. Would we be content with an omelette? After we had had a wash? It was to be regretted that neither houses nor hotels in the village had hot running water. Running cold water, yes – in plenty. And as much hot water as we wished, if we did not object to having it in an ewer.

As we opened the window and leaned out, there was complete silence except for the ripple of the running river.

The hotel was very small, which gave the proprietor and his wife more time to dedicate to the comfort of their guests, however late they arrived. The omelettes were delicious, and we ate to the sound of opera. The throaty notes of *Carmen* provided a Spanish background to Luxembourg bread, Ardennes ham in the omelette and Riesling-Sylvanus. Eventually we discovered that the gilt wall-clock was really a cunning loudspeaker broadcasting Luxembourg radio.

After our meal we walked round the town. The phrase is specifically accurate, but it needed the daylight to confirm it.

In the late evening there was almost absolute silence, a complete
lack of movement. Everyone was either in bed or listening with
doors and windows shut to *Carmen*. The only sound, enhancing
the tranquility, was an occasional leaping of fish by the dam.
When we had circled the town we climbed the steep street to
the craggy ruins of the castle, and then walked with echoing
footsteps through the square to the river once more. It was not
only the most peaceful evening of our tour; I doubt if we knew
such enfolding silence in the whole of the following year.

There were perhaps half a dozen places on this trip to which
I would go back at a moment's notice. Esch-sur-Sure is high on
the list. I commend it without reserve to anyone who is weary
with the ulcerating tensions of their everyday world.

Next morning I climbed the wooded hillside opposite the
hotel. Paths were well marked, for this is walkers' country, but
I only wanted to reach a point where I could see the village
below. Other towns – Luxembourg and Besançon, for instance
– are built in the curve of a river, but Esche seemed unique
both because it was so tiny and because the loop of the river
almost completely encircled the hill on which the village was
built. The census gives the population as 350, and even when
the hotels are full it is not doubled. The villagers live in grey,
russet and peach-washed houses round the base of the hill and
along the little lanes leading up to the church, the castle and the
square.

The ruined castle's most notable inhabitant was a crusading
knight, who brought back from the wars a Saracen's head, and
I asked M. Neckar-Ney's son about it. A student in Paris, he
was spending the summer helping in the hotel.

'It is a very famous head. A very fierce one, so they say who
have seen it.'

'*Seen* it!' I must have sounded astonished. 'Is it preserved
somewhere?'

'Oh, no. It hung outside the castle gate for centuries. Then, one night, it disappeared. They say it appears again before disaster strikes our country.'

'Have *you* seen it, Jean?'

'I was too young. The invasion was over when I was born. But there are those in the village who say it appeared the night before the Nazis invaded Luxembourg. Just as it had done in the days of the First World War.' He laughed cheerfully, the gleam in his eye the reflection of a new age of computers and pop-music. 'It's probably what you call an old widow's tale. But you've seen our village. It's a long way from the rest of the world. Even a Saracen's head might appear in a place like this!'

I asked the hotelier if it was possible to cash a traveller's cheque; if there was a bank. He smiled and directed me down the road. I understood the smile when I reached the house. The only bank in Esch-sur-Sure was a gentlemen's hairdresser's. The elderly barber, with a comb and scissors stuck in his breast-pocket, scuffed at the back of a drawer which had hair-clippers and cut-throat razors at the front. The notes he pulled out – Belgian, French, Italian, Austrian, German – were held together with elastic bands.

Possibly he had a larger supply in a well-hidden safe. But it seemed to me that nothing could be more typical than this hairdresser of a lovely village where the only prowlers in the darkness of the previous evening had been the cats – and ourselves.

Find Esch-sur-Sure for yourself. It is worth the detour from the wooded road to Ettelbruck and Remisch. And yet, per-haps, the right time to arrive is when we did ourselves. As we passed the Barrage of the Sure in the morning the first coach-tours were beginning to arrive.

4) *Grand Duchy*

THE ARDENNES, where Shakespeare placed his 'exiles' instead of the more familiar Arden, have been the camping-ground of the armies of Europe from the days when Roman legions marched this way and the historian Pliny sampled their delicacies with epicurean pleasure, to the time when the Nazi tanks rolled out of the sheltering woodlands towards Bastogne. That there should now be an independent country, compact and proud, which bears the grandiloquent title of the Grand Duchy of Luxembourg, is a tribute to a people with a strong sense both of destiny and history.

Luxembourg is a sovereign state with just over 300,000 people living in an area of almost exactly 1,000 square miles. Which is enough statistics to be going on with for the time being.

Probably few readers want more history than can be provided in two lines, but to do justice to the people of this gallant country there must be more than that. Ettelbruck, the first town we came to after our early picnic lunch, is not only an excellent touring centre but is also, in itself, a synopsis of the whole span of Luxembourg history. It holds a statue linking the country with the last war, while its very name takes us back to Attila's Huns who shattered the crumbling remnants of the ancient Roman Empire.

Ettelbruck means 'Attila's bridge' for the 'barbarians' (Huns, Vandals, Goths and Visigoths of the school history books) once rode their squat ponies through the tracks of these same forests. Before the Huns there were the Romans, and before them the Ligurians and the Celts. The real origins of the nation, how-ever, are found some centuries after Attila had passed with his barbaric warriors.

In A.D. 963, on April 12th or 17th (the date on the parchment is blurred) Sigefroi, the youngest Count of the Ardennes, was granted certain lands by the Abbey of St Maximin. The grant included the ruins of a Roman fort above the Alzette. Few nations can date their emergence into the modern world so explicitly and the parchment, one of the greatest treasures of the Duchy, can still be seen. Sigefroi carved out new lands for himself, having rebuilt the Roman fort, and to his new, per-sonal empire gave the name 'Lutzelburg'.

In 1963 the Luxembourgers kept festival and invited the world to celebrate with them a thousand years of unbroken nationhood. Yet, with its thousand square miles of woodland and good earth, this is no real-life Ruritania, no synthetic creation like tiny Liechtenstein. Nor is it an anachronism in the world of Great Powers. It maintains its position in the modern world by right as well as history.

There is no need to follow the story in detail. Its early over-lords squandered their fortunes and then sought to recoup them by plunder on the Crusades. Failing in this they were reduced to bankruptcy by reckless living, and it was a woman who re-established the prestige of the state. The Countess Ermesinde, in the 13th century, reformed the laws, advanced the good of the common people and granted charters to

Luxembourg and other cities. A century later the tiny state made a bid to dominate all Europe when its ruler, Henry VII, was manoeuvred on to the throne of the Holy Roman Empire. His son, John the Blind (whom we were to meet again in the capital) carried his conquests from the Carpathians to Crécy; and Wenceslas ruled from Muscovy to the North Sea, from the Baltic to the Alps – a territory five hundred times the size of the present Duchy. Yet soon afterwards Philip the Good, Duke of Burgundy, bought the state from its impoverished ruler in exchange for a gift of hock. For four centuries after that Luxembourg was ruled by a series of 'outsiders' who reflect the balance of power in Europe. Burgundy . . . Spain . . . France . . . Spain . . . Austria . . . France . . . Prussia . . . Holland. Not until 1867 did this dispiriting era come to an end. Then, by the treaty of London, it was accepted that 'the Grand Duchy of Luxembourg forms a free state, independent and indivisible'.

Ettelbruck takes us to the end, as well as the beginning of the invasions, for General Patton, the United States Army Commander, has an honoured statue here. Luxembourg was in the 'hot zone' of the war from 1940 onwards, and for its people the war, even at its coldest, was never as 'phoney' as it appeared to the rest of the world. On 10th May 1940, Nazi forces overran the whole country. The Royal Family and the Government escaped, to continue organising resistance. But, within the country, 16,000 Luxembourgers were taken away to prison or concentration camp.

Not all of them returned.

Beyond Ettelbruck is Colmar-berg, the summer palace of the Court. There are dozens of other castles in the state, though they lie to the north, and with castles in plenty ahead of us we did not turn off to view this one, which is not as handsome as Wolsey's Hampton Court nor a tenth as dignified as Windsor.

Besides, we had an appointment in Luxembourg at 3 o'clock.

The capital itself astonished us, though it should not have done. It is, after all, not a bit of ancient history clinging precariously to the modern world, but a full partner in the Benelux consortium of nations and a member of the Common Market. It is not the Ardennes which are most important here, but the country's coalfields and iron-plants. You cannot forget that the Headquarters of the European Coal and Steel Authority are located here. Yet, even so, the cosmopolitan sophistication of this thousand-year-old capital *was* surprising. In many places economy is closely tied to tourism, but not even the flimsy publicity brochures supported this impression in Luxembourg. The city exists for itself rather than its casual visitors – yet no town, or country, gives you a friendlier, if self-possessed welcome.

It is a place of wide boulevards, trees, parks, modern buildings which are functional without being *outré*. Its streets abound in long-finned American-type cars and sprightly dark-eyed people, both moving purposefully and fast. The well-dressed young men and pretty girls had none of the sallow, hollow-eyed weariness of London-by-escalator commercial crowds. They were never too busy to smile.

Yet, surrounding this square mile or so of international life, the narrow lanes, crooked buildings, steep gorges and deeply-hidden fortifications of the old town hem it in and claim it, in part, for the past.

Our mid-afternoon appointment, however, was within the modern world.

In much of northern Europe, 'Luxembourg' means only one thing: a familiar wavelength on the transistor radio, and endless outpouring of 'pop' music interpolated with smooth invitations to buy, buy, buy. From outside, Radio Luxembourg is a neat white block, a square tower, some attractive gardens. Inside, it is smaller than you anticipate. Commercial radio, most of it on tape or disc, needs only a handful of people to run a programme – as long as they are prepared to work, and go on working.

We were greeted, without either formality or enthusiasm, by a pleasant young man with an Australian accent. Luxembourg disc-jockeys spend a good deal of the day preparing scripts, long hours sitting before the microphone – and fill in the summer afternoons taking tourists round the works. Under questioning from three teenage girls, this one admitted his identity.

'My name is Moran.'

The teenagers gaped. '*Johnny* Moran?'

'That's me.' The smile was momentarily photogenic. 'Johnny Moran, your Music Man.' The smile switched off again. 'I've been asked to show you round.'

The tour was brief because there was little to see, as if the BBC Television Centre and Broadcasting House had been rolled into one and then squeezed down to almost nothing. A smallish concert-hall, a few TV stages and a series of cabin-like radio studios, representing a dozen languages between them. Offside, there were undoubtedly offices where the fan-mail was counted, the postcard 'requests' sorted and the cheques stacked. But that was all.

We thrust into the small studio which would later be sanctified by the D.J.'s presence . . . looked at the turntables, the tape-player and the microphone . . . and began to ask questions.

'Do you *enjoy* this?'

'Oh, yes.' Honest enough but no thrilling overtones.

'How long do you work?'

The answer was not very explicit. Counting the time spent on the script, sorting out requests, keeping in touch with every new release and the position of all the 'discs' in the British, American, Australian, Belgian, German 'top twenties', and then actually broadcasting, it sounded like all day and half the night. Perhaps it was meant to sound like that.

'What's going to happen if we get commercial radio in Britain?' we asked.

'I don't know what would happen to Radio Lux,' said Mr Moran, 'but your Music Man would be in the queue for the D.J. desks. It's a bit restricted here. It would be nice to live somewhere bigger than the Grand Duchy instead of having five weeks holiday a year.'

He gave us a television smile, said 'Goodbye and good luck' and went back to work. Personally, I was surprised that he could smile at all.

Our hotel, in sharp contrast with little Esch-sur-Sure, was situated in a narrow street of small shops selling sausages and cooked meats. An undertaker was a couple of doors away, with coffins even bigger and more ornate than Bruges'. The outside of the hotel was brown-painted and unpretentious; the restaurant check-clothed and ordinary. In such tourist hotels, however, there is no compulsion to use the restaurant at all. You pay for your room and bed, that is all. To buy rolls and butter and make your own coffee by the roadside would work out cheaper than the hotel's continental breakfast and no one worries about it. The first consideration, therefore, must be the bedroom – mattresses, hot water, toilets, linen. If these are not up to standard you may cancel your reservation – though you are not very likely to get your booking-fee back. Not that we had any complaints to make; however dull below, above stairs everything was adequate.

I have always found that the first most useful source of information about things to do and see is the hotel itself. This time, however, the hotelier was not in evidence, the waitresses were dumb and not one likely to impart any gossip sat having a lonely drink. Even so, exploring it by the guide-book and our noses for the unusual, we found Luxembourg one of the cleanest, friendliest and pleasantest towns in Europe.

Its situation is impressive for it stands high above a loop in
the river. On one side the hillside sweeps down to a wide
valley now filled with the 'lower town'. On the other, from
the Place de la Constitution, you look across a deep gorge cut
by the river Petrusse and spanned by two splendid bridges.
Today, however, the gorge is filled with trees and gardens,
while the Petrusse has suffered sadly from modern drainage
systems. It is no more than a sad little trickle of water, confined
to an open concrete drain two feet wide.

In the wide *Place*, filled with people, we heard little English.
The natural language here is Lutzeburghische, a tongue based
on middle German, with borrowings from Saxon, Latin,
French and Celtic. But the official language is French. School-
ing, however, begins in German, and French is added a little
later. In High School there is a choice of compulsory English,
Spanish or Italian. It is not surprising that few Luxembourg
girls take *au pair* jobs to learn English, and that a considerable
number find work as high-speed secretaries and translators in
the multi-lingual international organisations.

Through the years the suburbs have spread down into the
valley and across beyond the gorge. The old city itself, linked
with the newer town by the splendid Adolphe bridge, the
Viaduct and Pont du Chateau, is concentrated on the very edge
of the precipitous cliffs. The oldest part is comparatively small,
and we took only a few minutes to walk from the Place de la
Constitution through the rue Notre Dame, past the Town
Hall, the Atheneum and the cathedral to the fish-market and
the Grand Ducal Palace. Behind the palace is the Bock cliff.
There must be few towns more magnificently sited.

That it stands amongst the natural fortifications is not, of
course, accidental. It was colonised by the Romans – perhaps
on the camping grounds of more primitive peoples – and one
of their 'remains' holds its special place in history. This is the
base of the tower known as 'the Broken Tooth', originally par

Radio Luxembourg

Rothenburg-ob-der-Tauber: The Plonlein

Oberammergau: Fresco

of the Roman fortifications. The tower itself is the only thing
to be seen of Count Sigefroi's first city.

I have already written of this young count who created the
state of Luxembourg a thousand years ago. But legend must
have its share with history. How did one man manage to create
a city so impregnable in so unlikely a place? Some of the folk-
tales assert that Sigefroi sold his soul to the devil, who built the
city in a single night. The more romantic tell how he fell in
love with a beautiful girl, a stranger, who gave him the magi-
cally created city as a wedding gift on condition that she had
Saturday to herself, without interruption. Naturally, after years
of tolerance, the count became suspicious that there was a
handsome gigolo somewhere who also had Saturday off.
Following her he found that she only made her way to the
river Alzette, which still flows below the Bock cliff. There, she
slipped off her clothes, slid into the river and climbed a rock
where she sat and combed her hair. Only then did he recognise
her as the river-maiden Malusine. His foot dislodged a stone as
he turned to hide in the trees and his wife caught a glimpse of
him. At once she plunged into the river and was seen no more.
In the one story he lost his soul and in the other his wife.
Luxembourgers would insist that, in both cases, he kept the
most important thing – the city.

The cathedral has its own link both with England and Wales.
In the high-vaulted building made delightful by its uncluttered
simplicity – contrasting nobly with the gold and white baroque
of Bavaria and the dusty shrines we found in France – stands
the mausoleum of John the Blind, Count of Luxembourg and
King of Bavaria.

Unable to keep this bit of complicated historical knowledge
to myself I explained that the Luxembourg count was also king
of Bohemia because he was the son of the Holy Roman Emperor.

'But the Romans were here centuries before the first count
was born!'

D

'That was the Roman Empire . . . the *Holy* Roman Empire was in the middle ages.'

'But—'

I interrupted the argument, too complicated to interpret, with more information. 'He was killed fighting against the Black Prince and the chivalry of England.' That sounded very 'ham'. The history lesson was not going well.

'They can't have been very chivalrous to fight against a blind man!'

'It was only because his army was losing that he was in the fight at all, lashing about with his great long-sword. . . .' That was 'ham', too. I gave up. 'The Black Prince said the victory was not worth the death of so great a man.' That, at least, the history books recorded, and light dawned.

'Oh . . . Crécy?'

'Yes. 1346!'

'And the Prince of Wales's feathers?'

'Right again. The Black Prince may have regretted John's death, but he still took the blind Count's coat-of-arms for his own. And his motto, too. *Ich Dien*. The motto and the plumes have belonged to the Prince of Wales ever since.'

The tomb is worthy of a great man.

We were undecided whether to eat in the dull dining-room or go out, but as it happened, the problem was solved for us. The waitress was apologetic.

'If you don't mind waiting . . . it may be a long time . . . we have a Club.'

'What sort of club?'

She shrugged at my ignorance. 'A drinking club, naturally.' We caught a glimpse of them as her colleague elbowed the door open, a clutch of wine-bottles against her bosom. The Club appeared to have been in session for some time. Deciding against temporary membership we went out to find dinner at the *Schintgen*, and were confirmed in our estimate that Luxembourg is one of the cheapest and best places to eat in northern Europe. We had a sustaining local soup, duck whose flavour had nothing of the poultry-factory about it, and a Moselle which was a reminder that we must stop at the frontier to see the wine-cellars at Remisch. It was a friendly meal, enlivened by a clucking and cooing from the dining-room staff in the corner. Unable to contain themselves, they came across with a handful of pictures.

'You would like to see, no?'

We could only say 'Yes', and ask what they were.

'The daughter of *monsieur le proprieteur* was married. The photographs have just come.' The waiter swept away our empty plates, dusted the table of crumbs. 'If Madame pleases.' The white cloth was snowed under with pictures.

Very charming they were, if rather self-conscious and formal. But even more delightful was the readiness of these happy people to share their pleasure with someone they would never see again. Their ability to make the guest feel wanted was not so much a skill learned from experience as a spontaneous *bonhomie* which was entirely uncultivated. As much as anything, it is such natural friendliness which would make me choose the *gasthof* in preference to the hotel, the lower rating rather than the higher. I am left wondering why so many people pay so much for the veneer when the natural is so much cheaper and memorable.

Walking round the town after our leisurely dinner we found the main buildings illuminated. From the Adolphe bridge the view is entrancing, and the twin spires of the cathedral, needle-slim, pierced the dark sky. The Grand Ducal palace, illuminated too, but invisible from the bridge, had a huddle of shops and houses built right round it, very democratic indeed.

Democracy is the keynote of Luxembourg.

There is universal suffrage over twenty-one, and the Cham-

ber of Deputies has a member for every 5,000 people. It is a
democracy in which the ruler may propose legislation and, if
she thinks that a law is a bad one, may send it back to the
Chamber to be thought through again. The system works
admirably – perhaps because of its ruler. There was hardly a
window-display where the photograph of the Grand Duchess
Charlotte was not surrounded by a fresh posy of flowers,
delicately arranged.

Charlotte's path to the throne was a curious one. The Grand
Duke Adolphe, Duke of Nassau, who came to the throne in
1890, was succeeded by his son William IV. Because of ill-
health he readily allowed his wife, the Duchess Marie Anna
de Braganza, to act as the real ruler. In 1912 their daughter,
Marie Adelaide, succeeded to the throne. Seven years later,
democracy was vitally tested. The unhappy Marie Adelaide
offered three choices to her people: to become a republic; to
continue to be ruled by herself; or to elect her sister Charlotte
as ruler. Overwhelmingly, Charlotte was elected to the throne.
Nearly fifty years later the national mood remained unchanged,
and ribbons in the national colours draped the photographs of
the only royal family in modern Europe which has kept its seat
by nation-wide popular vote.

Near the town hall we heard the sound of revelry by night.
The loud voices were vigorously tuneless, and coming nearer
across the square. The first two or three men weaving their
unsteady way, were followed by a long line of others. Hands
grasping unsteadily at hips or waists in front of them, twenty or
thirty inebriated citizens performed a hilarious cake-walk towards the town hall steps – a hazard that almost, but not quite,
brought disaster. As the last one reached the bottom we could
scarcely stop ourselves cheering.

We would evidently have had a long wait for our dinner.
The gay revellers who had just reached the bottom step and
were doing a sort of Luxembourgois 'Knees up, Mother Brown'

were the members of the 'club' from our hotel. It must have
been quite a profitable evening – for the hotel.

Few guide-books mention Hamm and, coming upon it
unexpectedly the next day a mile or so beyond the city it was
terrible and heart-rending. No tourist attraction, certainly,
though for many American families it is a place of pilgrimage.
Radiating from a mast where 'Old Glory' hangs, its stars and
stripes brilliant that morning against the cerulean sky, are count-
less arcs of white stones. Every stone is a cross. Every cross an
identical memorial to a young American who died in the last
months of the last war. Apart from its associations it is a lovely
place. The great stone columns flanking the steps carry coloured
relief maps of the battle-fronts and beyond the flag is a small
quiet chapel, a place for prayer and sometimes, no doubt, for
tears.

There is nothing morbid, little sentimental here. Only the
dignity of the Services . . . a restrained pride . . . a peace that
strikes the heart with anguish . . . and unending lines of crosses
reaching to the skyline. We shall not forget it.

From Hamm we swept quickly to the frontier. Remisch, the
frontier town, is a place of some charm, with wide tree-lined
promenades along the riverside.

Our own objective was the *Caves* of St Martin, the wine-
cellars the guide-books recommend everyone to visit. At the
main office a surprised face looked up from a table loaded with
meat-filled rolls and a *stein* of beer.

'Sir?'

'We have come to look at the wine-cellars.'

The face looked doleful. 'M'sieur, I regret. You could perhaps come back at two o'clock. Everything closes at twelve!'

5) *Without the Prince*

THE MOTOR-COACH which we had been following thudded to a halt and its cheerful complement of children came bundling out of the door. The girls, with flaxen plaits, and the boys, fair hair cut *en brosse*, all aged about ten or eleven, were already making for a gate into the woods as we drew up behind.

The village name-sign said 'Orchultz' but nothing on our printed itinerary suggested a stopping-place, and we would never have paused but for the children. As it was, the last of them had disappeared by the time we reached the gate. Now, however, lovely wooden signs caught our attention – a carved direction-post . . . a wooden boat atop another post . . . a carving of a Roman gladiator and another of an eagle. Stubbing our feet against the roots of ancient trees, entranced by the scent of the pines and lured on by the distant children's cries, we walked a few hundred yards and came in sight of a log-cabin, German pattern. Just beyond it the land fell away in a deep mountain slope of dark green tree-tops. We stopped and gasped. Ahead of us was the far distance of the Saarland and, immediately below us, the Saar itself. If the distant view was superb the more immediate one was spectacular, for this is the 'Saar bend'. Once more the configuration was that of Esch and Luxembourg, a gigantic loop in the river. In the far past, the water had laboriously cut its way through the deep pine-covered hills towards the cliff on which we stood. Defeated in its attempt to eat away the base of the precipice it had turned reluctantly back on its tracks in an immense loop.

It was a magnificent spectacle, not to be missed. Yet but for a coachload of eager children we certainly *would* have missed it. As we turned back from the gorge we had to step smartly aside to avoid half-a-dozen eager boys leaping like goats downwards to the foot of the cliffs.

Rebuffed by the custodian of the Moselle wine-*caves* we had made for the frontier – a real frontier this time where a smartly dressed Luxembourg soldier saluted us and waved us on to the burly German down the road. What happened, we wondered, if one got caught in this 'no man's land'? About a week later we found out! As it was, the German officer briefly inspected our essential green insurance card and wished us a happy vacation without even a stamp on our passports.

There is little doubt that the best way to see Germany is by car, though Bernard Newman, the best-seller travel writer, used a bicycle – with which you see less, but more intimately. If you walk you have time to see very much more of still less! There are trains, of course, but their main purpose is to take you from here to there. On continental trains the faster you travel the more you pay. There are 'supplements' for expresses, while the diesels, the fastest of all, have first-class only. Without a car, the most rewarding means of travel are the buses and, where possible, the post-buses. Everywhere you are likely to be treated helpfully. Outside the big towns, that is. But 'big towns' everywhere are the same – every man for himself, and if you ask the way it is always of a stranger! I can only say that

everywhere we went in Germany we were treated with
exemplary courtesy. It was true even of the roads. Or it may
simply have been that the 'GB' plate made national drivers
keep a safe distance.

Our 'first-day jitters' had quickly dissolved. The morning
call of 'Keep right!' as we left the hotel, repeated after coffee
and lunch stops, was normally caution enough. Coming off
side-roads or pulling out from a roundabout were the main
hazards.

Only once did I look into the face of death. Pulling out from
a *gasthof*, after parking on the wrong side of the road, I set off
blithely on the left hand side. The driver coming towards me
opened his eyes and mouth widely at the same time and we both
stopped violently. What he said was in German. Low German,
I suspected. Then he saw the GB plate, stopped what he was
saying, waved his hands in despair, made the sign of the cross
and waited for me to draw back from his bumpers. He was
still sitting there when we turned a corner two hundred yards
farther on.

The road, after we had left the Saar bend, opened after a
while into a splendidly speedy *autobahn* and, though we normally had no wish for speed, this time the opportunity was
welcome. Late starting as usual – every day there was always
shopping or something to be seen before we left – we had no
wish for sightseeing. Heidelberg lay ahead.

Of course there were distractions. Broad exits and the guide-
books invited us to the Saarland towns.

Saarlouis – 'where a tablet in the Bier Strasse marks the birthplace of Napoleon's general, Marshal Ney'.

Saarbrucken – 'university . . . Schloss Kirche (15th cent.) . . .
Johannes Kirche (Gothic, tower 266 ft) . . . Castle (restaurant,
15th cent.)'.

Homburg – 'Castle (18th cent., ruins, orangery and bearpit)'.

Landstuhl – 'climatic resort noted for peat baths'.

Kaiserslautern – '(Stiftskirche, three towers)'.

All very fascinating. But we suspected there would be no bears in the bear-pit and no oranges in the orangery. We did not want a peat bath and we were due for a surfeit of churches.

Besides, we had had no lunch.

The autobahns have many things to commend them. One is their engineering, with long twists and turns, uphill climbs and downhill sweeps that make them remarkably unlike our own motorways. Another is the absence of those huge ubiquitous signs which disfigure French and Italian motorways, advertising chianti, byrrh, sewing machines and *AGIP supercortemaggiore*. The lay-bys are one of their most pleasant aspects, running into the 'scrub jungle' which so often edges the road. It was into one of these that we at last drew off for lunch. A concrete table; rustic wooden benches; shade if you wished to avoid the sun. Thus Germany provides not only for foreign visitors but for its own travellers who take their eating as a serious business even in the open air. Britishers may criticise German discipline and regimentation, but the country lacks litter-louts. In Britain there would be more rubbish, and the furniture would not last so long.

Lunch over, we went walking in the woods and soon found it was well not to stray too far from the road. Once more I had that 'Grimm's Fairy Tales' feeling which had overwhelmed me by the Saar Cloef. There was little wonder that Hansel and Gretel got lost. The tall trees, with deep brown or silver bark, rose high towards the sky, where the vivid blue was fretted by the jagged branches and sharp points of the pines. Underfoot the needles of last autumn, and long autumns before that, were thick and russet brown. With the road out of sight, and two or three paths offering their temptation of choice, one felt the eeriness of a man bewitched by a spell that urged forgetfulness and discovery. Every sudden break in the trees was an invitation to penetrate deeper into the forest. Five minutes, and the autobahn with the rushing modern world would be forgotten. Ten minutes, and you might try to find your way back in vain. A quarter-hour of searching for the right path and you would be inextricably held by the tall trees, irrevocably lost. The forest stretched for miles towards and beyond the horizon. Hansel and Gretel may have found the Gingerbread House. I felt sure I would only have come upon the witch had I gone much farther.

The transition from forested loveliness to the factory-land of the industrial Saar was brutal, especially after our leisurely progress through art-conscious Flanders and the last two hundred rural miles. It was Saturday afternoon, and as crowded as our own industrial Black Country. Yet, though we only paused briefly in Mannheim, that was a reminder that all is not industry, even in the materialistic Saarland.

Mannheim is, of course, the second largest inland port in Europe – the biggest is Duisberg – with nearly thirty miles of quays; the first city north of Basle to be placed firmly alongside the river Rhine. On one bank of the river are chemical factories, but it is the other side which is worth seeing, with its riverside parks and gardens. Its history is even more remarkable than its layout, and is enshrined in its name. 'Mannheim' means, not 'a man's home' but the 'Home of Humanity' – and the words should have capitals for behind it lies the German concept of intellectual adventure and religious liberty. At the end of the Thirty Years War the Elector decided to lay out a new town here by the Rhine. Its first citizens, drawn by hope of new freedoms, were to be refugees from the persecutions and religious intolerance of Flanders, Wallonia and Piedmont. Liberty of worship and conscience was guaranteed to all who came, and the influx of Protestant workers and craftsmen which followed laid the foundations of the prosperity which followed.

'Remember those signs by the roadside?'

Indeed we did. Considering the absence of hoardings the neat mauve or yellow signs were noteworthy. Each bore the identical silhouette of a church with a short spire and the words *Heilege Messe* or *Gottesdienst*, with times of public worship in the town or village ahead. Yellow for Catholic, mauve for Protestant . . . never competitive, the roadside signs were evidence of one man's dream come true. The Elector hoped for such a future when he gave his new town the grandiose name of 'The Home of Humanity'.

Beyond Mannheim the great transport roads criss-crossed, packed with colossal vehicles even on a Saturday afternoon. Gigantic direction-signs pointed to the heart of manufacturing Germany, to the rebuilt townships which, less than twenty years earlier, had still been only rubble and twisted girders after the war. But amongst the great road signs was one that seemed to spell magic.

'Heidelberg!'

A sigh, half-blissful, rose from the back of the car.

'The Student Prince!'

I tried to soften the disillusionment that lay ahead. 'It's terribly big these days.'

'How big is that?'

'More than 120,000 people, anyway.' Anyone who expects the Student Prince to be singing Romberg-like songs in a Romberg-like setting is booked for disappointment. The first sight of the magical-sounding city must have shattered the dreams of thousands of visitors every year.

Heidelberg has one unforgettable view. That is the castle, rising red amongst the trees, seen from the far side of the rose-red Karl-Theodor bridge over the river Neckar. With the red roof-tiles of the houses below it and the woods rising like a green back-drop behind it, it is romantic at any hour of the day. In the morning mist, or shimmering in the summer heat, and still more in the orange light of sunset, it is magical indeed. For the rest, the Student Prince's city does not exist.

Not, of course, that there is nothing worth seeing in this pleasant, sophisticated town. At least you should not miss the museum's greatest possession, the Altar of the Twelve Apostles, Tilman Riemenschneider's finest carving. There is a good deal to look at, even though little is remarkable. But what produces the sense of shock for the 'romantic' visitor is the size, the modernity, the jostling crowds. This is a 20th-century city, not a mediaeval one, prosperous and pleasure-loving, thronged with people, more of them attracted by the gay, expensive shops than by the Philosopher's Walk, the Great Tun or the oldest university in Germany. If you hope for 'picture-book stuff' you will be grossly disappointed. Accept it as a newish town built round the scanty remains of an old one largely destroyed by the French in the 17th century, and there is much to enjoy.

The Germans have a peculiar affection for it. Its charms have been celebrated by more German poets and writers than any other city. Heidelbergers claim that more artists have painted it than anywhere else in Germany – even though there hardly seems room for an artist to set up his easel! Even odder is the traditional reason advanced for this overwhelming national affection.

'It reminds us,' they sigh, 'of Italy!'

That seems to me to be plain nonsense.

If you know no German it sounds terribly risky to write to the Fremdenverkehrsverband. You can do it for any town, for it is the 'room-booking-bureau' and the Fremden-etc. did us very well by booking quiet rooms in a plain, comfortable hotel with plenty of parking-space at the back behind a locked gate. Even here we found no other Britishers.

Outside the front door the single-decker trams sounded like a fully-armoured regiment of Heidelberg's mediaeval soldiers breaking ranks, and we followed the tram-tracks on foot to the long Haupstrasse. The High Street was almost as narrow as its 15th-century predecessor, and the pavements more crowded than Oxford Street in the sales. Noticeably, there was a preponderance of young people – more than we saw in any other town – noisy, gay, café-conscious. And everywhere, of course, Americans; not only tourists but officers, enlisted men, wives and cars from the U.S. bases. Possibly it is the Americans who have helped to send prices rocketing, but it was certainly not only the Americans who were spending the money. Late on Saturday night many of the extravagently expensive shops were still open, and their customers were often German and many of them young. Indeed, the only places which were stolidly closed were the inns – and they had only shut in self-defence since it would have been impossible to squeeze anyone else in.

At the most notable of them all, the *Roter Ochse* – the Red Ox – the doors were shut and the shutters open. This traditional haunt of Heidelberg students is full of displays of club caps, duelling swords and evidences of how, until recently, a university student of character behaved. If you can get in (possibly better in the morning) it is a 'tourist must', for it has been run by the same family for three centuries and is registered as an historical monument!

Apart from the Castle, three buildings in Heidelberg deserve notice – the Church of the Holy Ghost (usually surrounded by market-stalls); Heidelberg's oldest private house, the Haus Ritter, now a hotel; and the university. This last may be a shock. The oldest German university, founded in 1386, it is no 'Oxbridge' with 'dreaming spires and stately halls'. It seems entirely to lack premises, halls of residence and ancient glories. Indeed, the sole 'attraction' to visitors may be the students' prison where the university carried out its own discipline with a sadistic abandon more appropriate to the castle governor punishing his prisoners.

The difference between this and, say, Oxford, is that students always lived in the town. There are no 'colleges'. German students apparently needed no 'gating' to keep them at their books. Their twin relaxations, apart from music, were duelling and drinking. Some of the 'student inns', each with its own 'club' have seen ninety generations of students sitting over their beer *steins*. In place of loyalty to the college there grew up a passionate loyalty to the 'club'. Old men treasure their club caps with their coloured ribbons, and sometimes their duelling-swords, with the same devotion that a 'blue' gives to his Boat Race oar, and they will still wear their club headgear fifty years after their student days are over.

By night the university buildings, illuminated with amber light, look decidedly more romantic than they do by day.

Knowing the sequel we should come upon next day I paused near the market-place of the old town to recount briefly the story of the Handschuheim quarrel.

'It was here that Friedrich von Hirschhorn killed his uncle.'

'Why?'

'They'd been to a party.'

'In one of the students' pubs!'

'Far from it,' I said. 'At the castle. And the Elector, Friedrich V, had given to Hirschhorn's uncle, Handschuheim, a splendid ornamental dagger. Both sides of the family were in danger of dying out, and one of them got a bit nearer to it that night. They quarrelled about the dagger and young Hirschhorn ran his sword through his uncle.'

'What happened to him?'

'He was ordered to lodge a certain sum – I don't know how much – with the university to pay the fees of poor students. He did, too.' We walked on, subdued. 'But you'll have to wait till tomorrow for the rest of the story.'

It was a pity we had no time to visit the castle next morning, for though it has been in ruins since the French burnt it two centuries ago it is still impressive, and the only thing that kept us away on Saturday night was the thought of the restaurant prices. Its most notable possession, of course, is the Great Tun – a barrel so big that it seems like a monstrous joke. Even lying on its belly it still needs a stairway built up one side to reach the top. But tradition has it that Perkeo, the castle dwarf, managed to drain it to the last drop on one legendary occasion.

The Tun was no joke to the subjects of the Elector. One of the taxes paid to him was a tenth of every man's wine harvest. Two problems were implicit in the tax. The first was what to do with the wine, since no vineyard would pay its dues in its best vintage. This was solved by the making of the gigantic wine-cask holding 200,000 litres. (Poor Perkeo!) The second problem was what to do with the wine when the tax was paid and the Tun was full. This one the Elector dealt with very simply. He used it to pay, in kind, the state and court officials who abounded in the castle. No doubt the little dwarf, so dear to the heart of the Heidelberger, had his share even if he never drained the lot.

The next morning was warm and hazy as we drove down to the river Neckar and across the old bridge. St John Nepomuk, the patron saint of bridges, did nothing to stop this one being bombed in the last war, but his statue, now restored, gazed benignly down on us.

The patron saint of Bohemia, too, he lived in the 14th century and was chaplain to Sophia, the queen. Wenceslas, her husband, suspected the pious woman of infidelity and when John Nepomuk refused to divulge what she had said in the confessional, the king had the priest bound and flung into the river from the highest bridge in Prague. Though no proof appeared of the queen's innocence and no divine intervention saved his life, something most startling was seen by the Czech onlookers. The third time he came to the surface the drowning priest was seen to be wearing a halo, all glittering gold, and in it were five gleaming stars.

Good St John wears it still, in Heidelberg, above the canal in Bruges, and on many a bridge in western and central Europe.

Below the bridge the river flowed gently in the morning mist. At such a time it was hard to imagine the spirits that might rise from its depths to strike at a careless or niggardly navigator – the Neckergeist and the Hakenmann. The Hakenmann was apt to appear without reason and drag an unwary boatman into the water with a sort of shepherd's crook during the winter months. That sailors believed in him there can be no doubt, for it was traditional good sense to fling a few logs into the river or leave a few silver coins on a rock in token of respect and propitiation.

Had we seen either of these gruesome spirits it should have been the Neckergeist, for he howled from mid-stream in high summer like a drowning man – and then clutched the would-be rescuer to drown him in his turn.

We saw no ghosts that morning. Instead, our gaze was held by the red castle amongst the woods, its outlines and colour softened by the gauze of the morning mist. For a moment or two, as we looked back, Heidelberg was, after all, the city of the Student Prince.

6)   *Valley – with Castles*

NOTHING COULD have been better for our spirits after the Saturday-evening jostle of Heidelberg's *Hauptstrasse* than the gentle Sunday calm of the *Burgenstrasse* – the 'road with castles' – winding through the Neckar valley close to the river. The 'romantics' will nowhere find anything more to their taste than this journey from Heidelberg to Oberammergau. If you end with a few days in a quiet Tyrolean village (and there are many such) the fresh air of the mountains will blow sanely through the tales of beautiful princesses, sorcerers, shepherdesses and brigand-barons which you will accumulate on the way.

When you sight the Odenwald over the bonnet of your car it is time to slow down.

The church-bells were ringing when we left Heidelberg, though not as many as we expected, for this is Protestant country. We heard them again as we sighted the next river-town, Neckargemunde – largely unspoiled if you keep the riverside camping-sites with their orange and blue tents out of your field of vision. Indeed, every town along the Neckar valley possesses a turmoil of narrow lanes and twisting streets;

E

a tumbling vista of tiled roofs in faded shades of red and ochre; sharp zigzags of steep steps; flowers in abundance in tubs and window-boxes. And, of course, there is no town without its castle, mostly half-ruined, all whispering with legendary voices.

The castle of Reichtenstein, at Neckargemunde, was the home of a predatory baron. He had a daughter – and which baron's daughter was not beautiful? – named Uta, whom he locked in the tower when he hunted daytime game in the forest and at night when he hunted travellers on the road. One night a face appeared at her window – that of a man worse than her father, Baron Bligger of Neckarsteinach, farther up the river. Dragged out by Bligger – could anyone think of a more gothic, villainous name? – she was carried off to his Schwalben-nest castle, the Swallow's Nest, and once more locked in a tower. She must marry Bligger – or starve! Bligger's orthodox sense of honour is remarkable!

But Uta had one friend whom I have not yet mentioned. Not a soulful knight to court her in her solitude, but a pet raven. Each day, like Elijah, Uta was fed by the raven on dainty morsels ravaged from Bligger's own table. Chagrined by his prisoner's reluctance to be starved into submission, the baron at last discovered the raven and tried to stab it to death. Instead, it flew at his face, pecked at his eyes, and Bligger the Bad toppled backwards to his death on the rocks below his castle.

What happened to Uta no one ever told me.

Neckarsteinach, Bligger's town which we reached next, has not one but four castles. Two, including the Schwalbennest, are in ruins; the others are inhabited still. Accurate historical evidence exists to show what their owners were like. They were genuine 'bad barons'. There is proof that they put chains across the river to hold up shipping for robbery, and that many of them were highway robbers and terrors to the river towns. Many were outlawed by the Emperor. One, however, despite being outlawed, joined the Crusades, turned his violence to pious account and even decapitated a Saracen leader. That he was pardoned by the Emperor is proved by his coat-of-arms in the church, on which he was permitted to display the Saracen's bearded, severed head.

Near to Neckarsteinach, though we had no time to search for it, is Dilsberg, the perfect fortified hill-village, almost hidden and quite unassailable.

Hirschhorn, a mile or so beyond Neckarsteinach, is the most picturesque of all the towns bordering the river. I will not try to describe each one, but Hirschhorn did make us pause.

It was the home of young Hirschhorn, who ran his sword through his uncle Handschuheim in the Heidelberg market-place.

'The Hirschhorn family died out in the 18th century,' I explained. 'But, if it hadn't been for that quarrel long before, it might have existed still. In 1830 workmen were making some repairs here in the Hirschhorn castle when they came on a cavity. As they moved a stone a lady's shoe dropped out. They began to dig more carefully until they opened up a space in the wall. Inside, in a hole just big enough to stand up in, was the skeleton of a woman.'

'She'd not just been . . . walled up . . . alive?'

'Presumably. But that's not the whole story. Sixty years earlier, in the old Handschuheim castle on the other side of Heidelberg they'd found the skeleton of a young knight, holed up in the same way, still dressed in armour. It was then that local folk recalled what had always been regarded as a legend . . . how two young people, the last in line of each of these families, had fallen in love and made up their minds to marry and so end the old quarrel.

'But their elders, the legend went, were determined that nothing should heal the breach. They would rather that each family should die out.

'And die they did. Each of them – in the walls of their own homes.'

We fell silent for a while. Then: 'What a horrid tale for a nice day! Let's get on!'

The sun came out again from the mist, and the river sparkled. The little, mediaeval towns dropped away slowly behind us.

Eberbach caught our fancy, not because of the Cistercian monastery or the wonderful old houses clustered by the bridge, or the Stolzeneck castle of the marauding barons. The interest was more contemporary than that. Half way up the hillside is a hunting-lodge, in reality another castle, whose owner is the Margrave of Baden, brother-in-law of the Duke of Edinburgh.

Zwingenberg, which we next saw, has a castle, of course, but is better known for its heronry. Once the river was the haunt of herons for many miles, but, like the storks in Denmark, the pace of modern living and the fowling-pieces of the hunters drove them away. Here at Zwingenberg they have been resettled, and now more than sixty pairs can be found living in protected peace in the heronry across the river. The water-spirit which once rose and broke the ice for them on the frozen river is needed no longer. Looking like the stilted men of Namur the herons can be seen fishing in the river, their only enemies the kestrel hawks. To save themselves trouble the hawks chase the herons who, in fright, regurgitate the fish they have swallowed while the swifter kestrels swoop below them and snatch the fish in mid-air.

Neckarelz, with its lovely timbered houses, was quickly passed and we did not stay to see the Guttenberg castle at Neckarzimmern where Gutz von Berlichengen lived, 'the knight with the iron hand'. We had coffee within sight of an old monastery by the river, where lazy-looking barges linked together in half-dozens swept up wide bow-waves in the green water. Now, with plenty of picnic food in the boot, we intended to stop in Heilbron – an imperial town, the largest wine-centre in the Neckar valley – only long enough to buy some bread and fruit. Instead, we pulled up on the main road near a modern, functional-looking building. Judging by the number of people moving in and out something was going on – and I was never one for seeing 'something going on' without trying to find out what it was. We locked the car, walked up through the flower-beds and looked inside.

Assuming it might be an exhibition, we went in. Nobody tried to stop us, but we were taken aback by the exhibits. The entrance-hall was full of deep-freezers. And the freezers were full of *Wurst*. There were frozen vegetables here and there, and frozen joints of beef. But they were overwhelmed by the sausages. Long thick sausages, long thin sausages, sausages as black as black puddings or white as milk, sausages the colour of blood. I was thrust by the crowd against a heavy, butchery-looking man.

'What is it?' I asked. 'What have we got mixed up in?'

'It's a Convention,' he answered. 'A sausage-makers' convention.'

Movement was, for the moment, impossible. 'It looks like a national industry,' I prompted him.

His gleaming face beamed. 'It *is* a national industry, *mein Herr*. How would we live without *Wurst*? It was we who taught America about frankfurters. A great town for sausages is Frankfurt. But wherever you go in Germany you find towns with their own speciality. *Fleischwurst* and *Rindwurst* and *Gelbwurst*. *Weisswurst* and *Bluttwurst* . . .' We were getting separated, but I could still hear his voice. '. . . and *Milzwurst* and *Mettwurst* and *Knackwurst* . . .' The voice faded, but as we made our exit after looking in the lovely concert-hall where there had just been a film – about *Wurst*, no doubt – I had a feeling he was still proudly reciting his catalogue though his audience had been swept away.

We looked with new eyes at those who were making their

way out beside us. Long thin men, long fat men, short red men, round white-faced men. I wondered what the men looked like who made *Mettwurst* and *Knackwurst*.

Back in the Cortina we avoided the sausage-makers' American-like giants and made for the open road. Now the Neckar was left behind and we pressed on to make our first contact with the Romantic Road. We were to join it halfway down its length, instead of at Nurnberg or Warzburg, where most long-distance drivers do so. Given the choice of the two routes I would hold out for the Neckar valley, where you have Schwabisch Hall to look forward to before the Romantic Road.

Not even the *Wurst* had put us off lunch and, after swinging upwards round a series of hairpin bends, we pulled on to a cart-track on the right-hand side of the road. It was one of our most inspired 'lucky stops'. Away to the north, across green meadows and dark forests, the horizon, lost in the heat haze, seemed almost an infinity away. One or two German cars had found the same stopping-place, but the cart-track wound on-wards for half a mile with wide grassy banks before it petered out by an old farm house. We lay in the sunshine after lunch, exulting in the warm air and the splendour of the view. Then, climbing slowly back to the high point by the road, we paused at the beautifully carved notice board. Its command, in gothic German script, read: 'Praise God, all the earth!' Nothing could have been more appropriate to our mood this Sunday. It took a good deal of resolution to pack up and leave.

Half an hour later we were in Schwabisch Hall, and wonder-ing why we had not come sooner.

This is dominantly Protestant country, and both Protestants and Catholics take their Sundays seriously. The shops were all closed, apart from a few cafés. The streets were almost empty and so was the large car-park. There were no coaches. The

town, in the summer air, was somnolent, with only its children
moving here and there in an ancient lane.

If much of this exquisite town remains as it has been for
centuries that is not because it has been preserved for the
tourist trade. In Rothenburg, to which we came next – and
which we love – there is something self-conscious in the preser-
vation of 'things as they always were'. When a film-unit found
the cobbled Rothenburg streets too uneven for their cameras
and asked permission to move some of the cobbles the city
fathers agreed only after long deliberation – provided every
stone was numbered and set back in its exact position. In contrast, Schwabisch Hall is a lived-in town. Yet even so it is a
mediaeval one, too, and much of it remains as it was five
hundred years ago.

From the car park we went down the narrow steps that led
to the river bank. At once our entrancement began. The river
ran slow and green, the bright sun striking flecks of gold from
the arrow-shaped ripples left by the swans. Across the river,
narrow grey houses with steep roofs flanked the water, their
wooden frontages bending outwards or backwards. Above
them rose a huddle of old houses and, from the river's edge, a
flight of steps twisted sharply between them. A child in a red
dress gave an additional flicker of colour to the tubs of flowers
standing in the angles of the stone stairway, while red, orange
and flame begonias and geraniums flashed bright against the
grey walls.

Two ancient wooden bridges spanned the river, one straight
and one dog-legged, with pointed roofs and overhanging eaves,
while rowing boats nudged their way between the supercilious
swans. We idled across the green lawns and then over an old
stone bridge. An immense wall and the river itself had provided both fortification and moat. Beyond the wall half-
timbered houses lined the streets, the living-rooms jutting out
above the shop-frontages. The high, crenellated wall of an old

mansion rose to a steep red roof broken by dormer windows.
A fountain gurgled gently in the square, where a boy in *Leder-
hosen* was dribbling his fingers in the cool water.

Susan and Paul went with my wife up the wide steps leading
towards the upper town, where the tower of the parish church
was a demarcation between the old town and the 20th-century
suburb on the hill, while I went hunting subjects for photographs. Before I found them again, drinking coffee by the riverside, the empty streets had become a babble of voices. Most
were women's voices, young and old, and the lanes were
crowded as the women poured down the stone steps. Amongst
them were scores in uniform – the uniform itself only the
remnants of mediaeval daily dress. With white starched caps
and long, deep blue dresses, a medallion on a silver chain proclaimed them to be Deaconesses of the Lutheran Church.

'It's the seventy-fifth anniversary of their college.' Susan
pushed the service-sheet across to me. 'The church was packed.
Some of them have just been ordained.'

The peaceful faces of some of the younger members of the
Order, as they wandered about with their sombrely-dressed
parents, still reflected the great moment of their lives when they
had made their vows in the parish church. But there was mirth
and a sort of rural exuberance amongst them, too.

'You should have come with us. The singing was wonderful.'

I wished I had done, if only because of the last hymn, for no
words or tune express the feeling of the German people like
Luther's *Nun danket alle Gott*. It transcends national and
denominational boundaries, and is as redolent of the Protestant
spirit as Luther's Bible itself. Surging full-throated from the
days of the Reformation it is as much a song of 'human rights'
as *We shall overcome*, and has served much the same purpose of
uniting the weak in face of tyranny and oppression. Hitler must
have hated it, for its echoes rolled out across the squares of
Oslo, Amsterdam and Copenhagen even while the jackboots of

his invading soldiers tramped the streets of the towns he believed he had conquered and subdued.

Here in Schwabisch Hall it nerved young women newly-dedicated, and older ones more tired, to face the challenge of a changing age.

7) *The Golden Griffin*

THE UNFENCED fields, golden with corn, edged the roadside and a hare loped across in front of the car without haste, for on this by-road to the *Romantische Strasse* there was hardly any traffic at all. Then, slowly, a low blur on the horizon, like distant land seen from the sea, began to take shape as towers and turrets and red stone walls. Looking exactly as it must have done to visiting Electors or the invading Swedish army whose conquest gave the town its most famous 'legend', Rothenburg-on-the-Tauber rose from the surrounding plain. Its walls were rose-pink in the summer sun. Its entrance-gate gaped beyond the moat, and its towers were as multitudinous as in a 16th-century woodcut. Beyond the two gates of the Spitalbastei, marked with the date 1572, we entered the best-preserved, least-restored mediaeval city of Germany. Two minutes later, at the top of the Schmiedgasse – 'the lane of the smiths' – we turned into an inn yard. We had arrived at the *Goldener Greiffen*. The elderly host, standing in the yard, bowed us into an open garage not so much as distinguished guests but as if we were members of the family.

'*Gruss Gott.*'

We exchanged the homely greeting of southern Germany.

'*Wilkommen!*' He clicked his old heels and introduced him-self. 'Sternkorb, Georg.' The letter replying to our booking, months earlier, had said: 'We wait to welcome you to our lovely city.' From the moment of our arrival we were at home.

From our bedroom, where the window-box was full of waxy begonias, we saw the golden griffin in its gilded iron-work high above the doorway of the ancient, narrow house with its age-darkened timbers. Below the *Gasthof* the narrow road sloped down to a gateway which might have been an intricately designed set for a film operetta. It is hard to believe that Rothenburg is real.

The *Greiffen* was not pretentious, and in the small entrance hall one or two locals sat with *Steins* of lager-beer. The court-yard where we had our evening meal was filled, late into the night, with Rothenburgers sitting over beer-and-gossip. There was no terrace to overlook the roofs and turrets of the town. But the house had an aura, an atmosphere that was apparent as we climbed the creaking stairs and emerged on to the wide, baronial landing with its spinning-wheel and its dark, deeply carved furnishings. From our windows, whose curtain-rails ended with wrought-iron rosebuds, we stared out at the house across the way, with the date 1551 traced on a wooden beam. Apart from the modern dress in the wide, cobbled square, flanked by the Rathaus and the Clock House, we might have been looking back over an unchanged four centuries.

It is no surprise that the *Greiffen* has the smell of history about it, for the very stairs we climbed and the open landing, once the guest-hall, had seen the nobility of mediaeval Rothenburg in constant traffic. Five centuries ago this was the house of Heinrich Toppler, who was born in 1408 and rose to be the most famous Burgermeister of Rothenburg's long history. It was here that he planned the extensions to the town, marked in new refinements on the architect's plans, entertained his royal masters and dispensed his charity to the townspeople. Rothenburg is still very much what he helped to make it, for, ever since, its burghers have resisted any kind of change. In earlier times this was no more than a rural conservatism. In the present century it is as much sense as sensibility. 'Let the tourist be served!' For artists and photographers the unchanged mediaevalism is both paradise and peril. Wherever you stand the picturesque is in view – delectable architecture, light, colour and detail – and yet you have a suspicion that round the next corner is a house, a gateway or a fountain which is yet more worth capturing.

The population is about 11,000, mostly Protestant, and since comparatively few new houses have been built inside the town over the past few centuries, the number of people within the walls cannot have increased very much over the years – though the present total includes those who now live beyond the old boundary. Rothenburg remains a completely walled city and from the walls, in every form of adventurous architecture, rise thirty-four towers. Its history goes back to the year 942 and beyond, for in that year reference is made to it in official documents. Two centuries later it was a Free Imperial City and, by 1400, was an important member of the Franconian League. By the 16th century it was prosperous by reason of its weaving industry. The next century it achieved its high peak of folk-history when it was captured by General Tilly and his Swedish mercenaries. After that, with Burgermeister Toppler's buildings still intact, the invading armies and the world passed it by. Like a fairytale princess, it seemed to go to sleep.

What reawakened it is difficult to determine. Bernard Newman asserts that it was a British artist named Seymour Lucas, a hundred years ago. The Germans claim that one of their own artists did so, considerably later. Certainly someone disturbed its mediaeval somnolence in the 19th century and, as a result, tourists flock into it from all over Europe and America. Strangely enough, most of them had either passed through it or gone to bed early when we were there.

Setting off from the *Greiffen*, we explored as much of the town as we could before dinner. Down first to the Spital-bastei, where the roadway snakes between two defending gateways to hamper any enemies who might breach the first bastion. In the car, we had gone too fast to see the inscription above the gateway, which might well have been written for us and our fellows as well as for the wayfarers of the middle ages.

> *Peace to those who enter;*
> *Good fortune to those who leave.*

The Plonlein, 'the little place' with the clock tower, must be one of the most-photographed subjects in Rothenburg, and we took its picture before coming back up the Schmiedgasse. Above the *Greiffen* – which the guide-books call the 'Topplerhaus', is the Baumeisterhaus, the House of the Architect, the home of Weidmann who built the present Town Hall. Outside the house are fourteen carved figures, the seven virtues and vices of classical theology. But the interior is more interesting than the outside, and for the price of a cup of coffee you can get in easily enough, for the Architect's House is now another hotel. The design is that of a typical patrician's home, and the restaurant is really the old carriage-way to the courtyard beyond, dignified and open to the sky, where coffee tables are now laid out. As in Toppler's house, the guests' staircase once led to the living-rooms on the first and second floors, while the top storeys were the granaries. Like the patrician houses of Flanders and the Netherlands the upper windows still retain the pulleys for hoisting sacks and stores.

The Schmiedgasse leads directly into the Marktplatz, dominated by the Rathaus, the town hall begun in 1572. It is in typical German renaissance style, backed by a tall tower. Here three elderly men, unseen by the passing crowds, keep lonely vigil.

The origins of the guard go back more than five centuries, to the days when the second Rathaus stood here. The first, built in 1240, had been burnt down. In the congested mediaeval cities fire was a constant hazard and watchmen were billeted in the new building to keep guard. Despite their 'vigilance' the new town hall caught fire on Ascension Sunday, 1501. The chronicler records that one of the guards was burned to death. The other, with his wife, hanged himself from one of the tower windows rather than wait the judgement which would certainly have awaited him below.

Fire still remains a peril, and the three men who carry out their eight-hour shift know it all too well. Not so many years ago a watchman fell asleep at his post and found to his horror that the tower was on fire. Little harm was done, but his successors have to ring the bell every quarter-hour to prove that they are still awake!

Though the interior of the Rathaus is open to visitors most people will prefer, as we did, to wander the old lanes – though they will certainly be in the square at eleven in the morning to watch the Burgermeister and the General go through their daily 'drinking bout' at the 'Drinking-hall of the Councillors'. Beside the Rathaus is the ancient chemist's shop, the Marien-apotheke, with the Herterichbrunnen, one of the town's most charming fountains, in front of it. The many lovely fountains all over Rothenburg are reminders that the mediaeval town was without any water supply within the walls. Underground pipes were laid in the 12th century to bring water from springs outside – and here, too, was another danger. In war the guarding of the water supply was as urgent as the fire-watch, and betrayal of its secret, properly known only to the Burgermeister and the 'water master', was treason punishable by death.

We 'wandered' until dinner-time, finding as much delight
in the quaint oriel windows, the ancient doorways, the ornamental timberwork and ironwork, and the varied gables as in
the views themselves. It is a town where detail repays a
watchful eye.

'You know this is the great Toppler's house?' Herr Sternkorb was hovering by us as we ate. We assured him that we did.

'Our greatest citizen. He even allowed ordinary people to
be members of the Town Council. It was he who gave the
Riemenschneider altar to the church. Have you seen it?'

'Not yet. But tell us about the "Master-drink". Is the story
true?'

Herr Sternkorb spread his hands in astonishment at our
doubts. 'But of course,' he assured us, his old eyes twinkling.

The details of the tale vary a little in the telling but the
chronicler, like our host, is certain of its essential truth. General
Tilly and his army laid siege to the city in 1631 but only succeeded in overcoming the garrison after a long and costly
assault. Angered at the long resistance the soldiers prepared to
make havoc of the town as the General rode into the Marktplatz and lined up the councillors before him, headed by
Burgermeister Nusch. Dusty and thirsty, the conqueror
demanded wine before giving the order to fire the town. It
was handed to him in a silver cup. He tasted, and drank
deeply. Then, so the story runs, he looked down at the
Burgermeister.

'How much wine does this cup hold?'

'More than three litres.'

'You make good wine in Rothenburg, Burgermeister. Do
you drink much of it?'

'I have done . . . in my time.'

'You have not much time left! But . . .' he laughed harshly,
'. . . if you can drain this cup at a single draught I'll spare your
city and your people's lives.'

With the wine spilling over its brim the cup was passed to the trembling mayor. He tipped it, hesitantly, and began to drink. Fear is said to narrow the throat. In Nusch's case it evidently distended it for, to Tilly's astonishment, he emptied the whole goblet without drawing breath. Perhaps to the mayor's surprise, the General kept his word and Rothenburg was saved.

'*Really* true?' we asked Herr Sternkorb.

'We have a play about it every Whitsuntide,' he answered. 'Ever since it happened. Besides, the very same goblet is in the museum.'

After dinner we went out again because we could not stay in. The sun was beginning to set as we looked at the town, watching its walls and turrets slowly change colour. It is at sunset that Rothenburg, the 'red town', is most memorable, for then the whole city catches fire from the last gleams of sunlight, glowing red from the towers and battlements. Even the mortar between the stones runs with the same colour and I noted the reason from a small book I picked up there. The secret lies in the mixture, so it asserts. The recipe: chalk, red sand, the white of eggs – and cottage cheese! If water was scarce in mediaeval Rothenburg, it seems that eggs and cheese were plentiful!

Where Toppler once kept his grain, we went to sleep to the sound of drinking songs and *Steins* clanging on the tables in the courtyard – and wakened refreshed to go shopping and visit St James's church.

The St Jacobskirche deserves more space than I shall give it. Without the stained lights of many French cathedrals or the golden baroque of the Bavarian churches, it is nevertheless an impressive building. A charming tradition is preserved by the 'marriage gateway'. Marriages were not blessed in the church itself but, passing through the 'marriage gate' the couples waited outside for the Church's benediction – within sight of

the world where they must live. The custom is still maintained.
But what everyone comes to see is the Riemenschneider 'Altar
of the Holy Blood'.

We saw it then in the south aisle, though it has now been
cleaned and moved, to its great advantage. It was carved in
1478. To Toppler's fellow-citizens the 'globule' of Holy Blood
shed on the Cross, enclosed in crystal and set at the top of the
altar-piece, was a priceless possession. To the moderns, with
less reverence for holy relics, the treasure of St Jakobskirche is
the carved altar-piece itself.

Tilman Riemenschneider's work is to be found throughout
the Tauber valley, much of it still in the churches for which it
was designed, despite the Altar of the Twelve Apostles in the
Heidelberg museum. Though we missed the most renowned,
that at Creglingen, farther up the Romantic Road, the Altar of
the Holy Blood made all the amends we needed.

At a period when few stonemasons produced masterpieces
to compare with the woodcarver's art, Riemenschneider was
the incomparable wood-craftsman of his time. In its exposition
of mood and character through the faces of these bearded 15th-
century Germans (for that is what the disciples really are) the
altar is both moving and heart-searching. The left panel of the
triptych shows Jesus arriving in Jerusalem, and the right in the
Garden of Olives. The central one displays the scene at the
Last Supper when Jesus announces that one of the disciples will
betray him. The panel itself is carved wholly from a single
piece of lime – an incredible four-year achievement, for the
carving is not a relief but a delicate sculpting of standing and
seated figures. Judas alone, either by design or as a result of
some accident in the carving, has been separately worked.

The great craftsman, according to tradition, was forced to
give up his work by an act of incredible malignancy. Born
amongst the peasants of the Harz mountains of Saxony, he
lived most of his life in Warzburg where he became a city
F

councillor and mayor. In 1533 there occurred the Peasant Rebellion. One of their objectives was the unassailable castle, the Warzburg itself, and it was with the connivance of Riemenschneider, whose sympathy lay with the peasantry, that the town was captured. He showed them a track leading to a lightly defended part of the wall. The peasants gained the city but not, in the end, the victory. The rebellion crushed, the sculptor was imprisoned within his own town. The horror of the story is that, by orders of the prince-bishop, his fingers were smashed and broken so that he could never again hold a wood-man's chisel.

From the dim interior of the church we came out into the bright July sunlight and made our way to the market place just before eleven o'clock. With the crowds from the incoming coaches we gaped upwards. The hour struck brazenly. Then, on each side of the clock in the Hall of the Councillors, small doors opened to reveal wooden busts of General Tilly and Burgermeister Nusch. Slowly each turned inwards. Nusch raised his goblet jerkily. Then they slowly dropped their arms as the doors closed. The show was over.

Yet, as we drove away, through the Spitalbastei with its inscription wishing good fortune to those who left the town, it was not of Nusch's great draught and an old deliverance that I was thinking. It was that this mediaeval gem might, like Nurnberg, have been reduced to rubble in the last war.

General Devers was planning an assault on the city with his American troops. Small though the town was he expected the usual opposition and was prepared to bombard it. By chance an American civilian at Headquarters knew the city and loved it. With some difficulty he persuaded Devers, to whom lovely towns were of less significance than victory, to spare the city if its surrender could be arranged. The visitor himself worked out the terms of surrender the next day, by agreement with the city authorities, and Rothenburg was declared an 'open city'.

That we are able to enjoy its beauties today is due to his intervention. His name was J. J. McCloy, and he was to become the United States High Commissioner in Germany. It was fitting that he should have been voted by the City Councillors an 'Honorary Patron of Rothenburg-on-the-Tauber'.

8)   *Romantic Road*

IT WAS likely to be a full day for, although we had only ninety miles to travel before we reached Augsberg, our route was the *Romantische Strasse*.

Though the road is almost as old as history, the name itself is new. Indeed, it did not exist before the last war. 'The Romantic Road' was the inspired invention of Dr Baumann, the Ministerial Director of the German Tourist Bureau. Reaching from Wurzburg to the royal Bohemian Castles and beyond to Fussen it covers some two hundred miles. It has been described (and not just in the publicity blurbs) as providing 'the concentrated essence of picture-book Germany' . . . 'a progression through a continuous, unbroken succession of marvels'. A rural road, punctuated every fifteen or twenty miles by exquisite and often unspoiled towns, mostly comparatively small, its passage could take you a week, though with 'improved' roads some people do it in a day – and see nothing. Even the names themselves are often magical or fantastical – Creglingen, Nordlingen, Dinkelsbuhl.

Twenty miles from Rothenburg we parked by an old

timbered inn in Feuchtswangen, to go and find the abbey
cloisters. It should have been easy. Round the corner from the
inn was the abbey church. But from inside it seemed impossible
to reach the cloisters. We walked round the church and found
ourselves back at the inn. Setting off a second time we watched
for a notice, but there was none. Despite the book, no one
seemed interested in these 'lovely cloisters attached to a convent
church'. Then we saw a narrow door, on the latch . . . stumbled
over some bundles of faggots . . . and were in the cloisters,
after all.

A bearded young man in jeans looked up and said: 'Shh!'
The pretty, dark-haired girl in a yellow sweater sitting by him
hardly glanced at us. A sharp, ringing voice echoed round the
cloisters. A woman with a stick angrily faced a youth at one
end of the enclosure. They relaxed as a tall woman, evidently
the producer, spoke from the arches at the farther side.

'What is this?' we asked.

The bearded young man was willing to talk now. '*Jedermann*.
The German *Everyman*. It's a great favourite with our audi-
ences.'

'Are you playing here?'

'For several weeks. Yes. There's a festival here each summer.
We're doing the *Merchant of Venice*, too.' He waved a hand at
the girl in the yellow sweater. 'Erna is playing Portia.'

Drama is a strong tradition in Bavaria and this part of
Germany. One manifestation is the folk-plays which, like *Die
Meistertrunk* at Rothenburg, are presented in many of the older
towns. Another is the Passion Plays, of which Oberammergau
is the most famous amongst many. At Feuchtwangen, during
July and August, a resident company performs in the cloisters.
Under the arcades, too, we found the *Heimatmuseum* with its
display of folk-art, and a shop full of charming souvenirs. The
tourist trade, German as much as foreign, has brought a new
prosperity to local craftsmen.

On the road again we crossed the river, and a signpost
pointed to Dinkelsbuhl. Not all names even on the Romantic
Road are so romatic. Schopfloch, for instance! But eight miles
after leaving Feuchtwangen we drove under a turreted archway in the ramparts and were in our second 'living mediaeval
town'.

Rothenburg . . . Dinkelsbuhl . . . Nordlingen – visitors will
argue endlessly which is 'best'. All three are completely walled
towns, though Dinkelsbuhl has only five gates and far fewer
towers than Rothenburg. Its moat is full, and swans glide in
stately procession. It, too, went to sleep in the middle ages.
Reawakened, it is busier and less self-conscious than Rothenburg, while Nordlingen is yet larger and still more 'lived in'.
If we preferred Rothenburg, and even Schwabisch Hall, it was
perhaps because we came to them first and were completely
captivated. Undoubtedly we gave both Dinkelsbuhl and Nordlingen too little time to absorb their unique atmosphere for
each of these towns demands at least a night, with an evening
and a morning to explore the narrow lanes and elegant houses,
of which both have their abundant share.

In St George's church, in Dinkelsbuhl, we found an altar
presented by the Shoemakers' Guild and dedicated to St
Crispin, the patron saint of shoemakers and cobblers all over
the world. It was well tended, with fresh flowers – a sign that
the old crafts have not yet been put out of business by mono-
poly-companies in Franconia and the neighbouring prov-
inces. On the church noticeboard was a poster advertising the
Kinderzeche, the Children's Festival. It took us back again to
General Tilly.

It was in 1632, the year before Rothenburg's deliverance,
that the invading army laid siege to Dinkelsbuhl. Its citizens
held out just as heroically, manning the battlements until it
became evident that not enough men remained alive or un-
wounded to resist any longer. But whereas in most towns the

Burgermeister would have sent a messenger to plead for clemency the councillors here hit on another scheme. When the town gates were opened no proud messenger in his civic robes appeared. Instead, a small boy marched out, followed by another, and another. One by one, the whole child population of Dinkelsbuhl walked solemnly out of the city gates towards the enemy camp. Emaciated and sick as they were, it was a splendid procession. Every child carried a branch of cherry blossom to lay as the city's offering before the astounded general. A man may make a mockery of a mayor, but he would be inhuman indeed if he took a sword to children.

That this is not legend but sober truth is substantiated by the fact that the *Kinderzeche* has been celebrated every year since then, except in times of disaster. Nowadays it includes dances, sword displays and a representation of the town's patron, St George, slaying the dragon. But it remains the Children's Festival, the cherry-tree fête, a gay memorial to an act of high courage.

Dinkelsbuhl retains its architectural character through the discipline of its city council. We saw a new house being built alongside an ancient one. The new building was tall and narrow, gable-fronted with long windows and a steeply-sloping roof. In the gable was the small window through which, in older houses, the grain would have been hoisted to the storeroom under the roof. Plastered outside, its windows bright with flowers, it would at a distance look undistinguishable from its neighbours. Dinkelsbuhl builds for the future, by public order, in the style of the past.

Outside the town the road was comparatively unencumbered by traffic, and the fields gave way to woodland. A shower of rain splashed from the blue sky, and we pulled in amongst the pines for our lunch. There were caterpillar-marks of huge tractors leading deep into the trees, and stacks of felled pines scented the air with resin. I walked away from the car as a treacly voice from the transistor wailed that 'summer time is swimming time'. Nailed to a tree-trunk was a notice and I went to read it.

'*Personnel*' – I remembered that here, like Heidelberg, we were in the overseas stations of the United States – '*are reminded only to swim in scheduled areas. Check with your bulletin board.*'

Despite the sugary invitation of the pop-singer I could not imagine why any service-man should want to swim in a pine-wood!

Nordlingen, our next stop, was a bigger and livelier town than either of its lovely predecessors, and more a part of the modern world. There are three things to do here, if you can. First, explore the battlements of the old city. We reached them up narrow steps by one of the town gates, where an artist was painting a twisted lane with the river beyond, and found them roofed and thatched, more to protect the sentries from enemy arrows than from the sun and the rain.

Then, you should walk through the market-place, where peasants from the surrounding Ries plains go about their business, unselfconscious in costumes that have been unaltered for hundreds of years. Finally, if you can, you should stay the night, for then the watchman goes his rounds, sounding the curfew. He calls all men indoors to leave the streets free of anyone except vagabonds and robbers, and announces the closing of the city gates. It is a useless custom, of course, since the city gates are now within the town and remain open, but no one would think of giving it up – any more than the wake-man and councillors of Ripon would give up the nine o'clock horn blowing which has continued for a thousand years.

We did not hear the curfew, but we did hear the old organ of the great town church, as a girl played it high above the nave. Yet more than the organ we shall remember standing behind the plain altar of this evangelical church. Round the walls of the apse were the stalls of the chapter, their stone seats placed there before the Reformation. And, above the stalls, score upon score of Iron Crosses, each with its own plaque and the name of the man it commemorated. The date on almost all these pitiful memorials of the futility of war was 1945, and almost every man was young.

Ten miles farther on a military helicopter flew overhead as we turned across a narrow bridge which spanned a thin stream trickling between muddy banks – the river Wornitz, soon to join the Danube. Beyond, poised in grim solitude on the edge of the wooded cliffs, was a dark, grim castle – the castle of Harburg. It was our last stop in Franconia, a province everywhere dotted with mediaeval cities. A small girl and a policeman in neat grey uniform edged with green were both leaning negligently against the bridge eating ice-cream.

'*Schloss?*' I asked, and followed the policeman's half-attentive directions round to the left, up a steep road to the castle, with a cobbled courtyard and untidy outhouses. Overhead the sky was going grey, making the castle greyer still, and heavy black clouds rolled across the outspread countryside from Augsberg.

'We'll get soaked,' said my wife.

'But we ought to see the castle. It has a library of 140,000 books and a great many Gobelin tapestries and a splendid collection of . . . of. . . .'

'Of what?'

I had left the book in the car and could not make up an answer in time.

As it turned out, it was of no consequence. Nobody came in reply to the clanging bell – though it was well after two o'clock. The new wing, which had been built on to the castle to house the treasures, seemed untenanted. In the car, I found that the book did not even say what it contained beside the tapestries and 140,000 books. We felt cheated all round.

Donauworth was a bit of a cheat, too. In the eighteen miles

from Harburg the rain began to fall. 'Donau' is the German for 'Danube' but Strauss was nowhere near Donauworth when he composed *The Blue Danube*. Under the lowering sky the river was almost black and we were convinced, even when the sky was cloudless, it would be no better than a muddy brown.

The great metropolis of Munich, says tradition, owes much of its importance to one of the faithful wives of this town. There was a time – and this is historic fact – when it was not only a Free City but was the capital of Bavaria. Its ruler, Duke Lewis the Severe, had a beautiful wife, Mary of Brabant. Unfortunately he believed her to be unfaithful and had her beheaded, only to discover convincing proof of her innocence soon afterwards. In anguish he sat all night by her tomb, stricken with remorse. Mary's tomb is still to be seen here in Donauworth, in a small chapel adjoining a school which was once a Benedictine abbey. But there is no memorial of her husband here. Anxious to forget his crime, the Duke of Bavaria moved his capital from Donauworth and set it up in Munich.

The next twenty-five miles provided us with a storm which, at times, was almost impossible to drive through. The sky was lowered with dense, black clouds. The lightning was incessant and the thunder sounded like celestial madmen hammering on celestial-sized tympani. Then, when we seemed likely to be blown right off the road, we ran most spectacularly out from the storm into bright sunshine – and into Augsburg. We stayed, appropriately enough, at a hotel for transients, the *Augsburger Sonne*. In the circumstances we should have been delighted with the city. In fact, that night, we found it uninviting and dull.

Our judgement was prejudiced and unfair. And all because we could not find a cup of coffee!

Augsburg bears the name of the Roman Emperor who

founded it in 11 B.C. – Caesar Augustus. It was already a
thousand years old when Frederick Barbarossa, the Red-beard,
came to it as Holy Roman Emperor, with three of his princely
sons and four bishops, bearing the remains of St Ulric to the
cathedral. The richest town in Europe in the 15th and 16th
centuries, it is now an industrial centre of importance. It is
astonishing to reflect that, though it now has a population of
almost 200,000, it had a population of 60,000 in 1660, which
made it a mediaeval metropolis.

Its roll of distinguished citizens has illustrious names – and
quaint memories. One of them conquered and owned the
South American state of Venezuela: Bartholomew Welzer.
Another, Solomon Idler, tried to fly a machine of his own
invention in 1635. By contrast Professor Picard was the first
man to reach the stratosphere – from Augsburg in an Augs-
burg-made balloon. Rudolf Diesel, who disappeared mysteri-
ously and for ever between le Havre and Dover, invented and
tested the Diesel engine here at the end of the last century, and
another inventor was Willi Messerschmidt, who had his aircraft
factory here. It was one of his machines, I was told, which first
broke the sound barrier in 1943. In the realm of creative art,
Augsburg boasts the home of Hans Holbein the Elder, whose
paintings are to be found in the cathedral, and Leopold, father
of Wolfgang Mozart, whose house behind the cathedral is a
Mozart museum. It is a town which should entrance any
visitor.

That night it did nothing for us. There were few people
about, in the centre. There were cinemas with bright lights . . .
open doors with invitations to cabaret . . . dim stairs down to
dubious 'dives' . . . beerhalls in plenty. But not a single café,
that we could find, ready to serve us with coffee. And, that
night, it was coffee we wanted. In the end we gave up, took a
tram for the hotel, could not remember the right stop, and got
off at the wrong place. I was not surprised when nobody

wanted to come sight-seeing with me next morning. Which
was a pity. I found none of the plum-tarts for which the town
is famous but, under cloudless skies, I discovered Augsburg to
be a place of great charm and with one wonderful claim to
fame.

At one end of the splendid Maximilienstrasse the town is
dominated by the Slav-looking minster of St Ulric. The tall,
slender tower with its onion cupola is a gracious end-piece to
the finest renaissance street in Germany. Like the much smaller
Holy Cross church, not far away, it is a 'twin church', for
though the main building is very evidently Roman Catholic
there is only a wall at the end of the nave to separate it from
the Protestant building which has been added to it. From the
front of St Ulric one is aware of the early town plan – a longish
axis comprising three streets – the Maximilienstrasse, the
Karolinenstrasse and the Hoher Weg. Matching the minster of
St Ulric at one end is the cathedral at the farther end of the old
town. Of the three great streets the Maximilienstrasse is the
most notable. Its homes are patrician, standing well back from
the pavement, stately and gracious. The road is immensely
wide and, like every Augsburg street, seemed calm and uncluttered despite the traffic. Everywhere I came upon fountains.
Augustus, Mercury, St George, Hercules, Neptune – all dating
from the 16th century. Full of elegance, classical figurines
clustering round them, they match the charm of the older
part of the city. Without waterspouts or rushing cascades, the
fountains play gently, plashing almost noiselessly into the
ancient basins.

From this same period is a more grotesque statue, dear to the
citizens' hearts – the 'Stone Man', now without arms and
having an iron nose where his stone one crumbled away. The
unrecognisable stone man was once a real man – a master-
baker who was so incensed when the Swedish soldiers who
later invaded Dinkelsbuhl and Rothenburg marched on his

town that he threw his last loaf of bread at them and was shot
for his patriotic gesture.

At the farther end of the Maximilienstrasse is the 'Perlach',
the tall 'Town Tower' rising behind the Town Hall. This
whole central area forms a tribute to one man such as few
towns can boast. Elias Holl, born in 1573, redesigned the centre
of his native city completely and saw it completed before he
died. Because of the immense and overriding powers vested in
him by the city fathers, and despite the criticism which broke
against his designs, Augsburg is his personal creation even more
completely than pre-blitz London was essentially Wren himself. The 'quaint' and 'picturesque' buildings which now
delight the visitor to the towns of the Romantic Road farther
north affronted Holl as unworthy of a great metropolis, as
Augsburg was in his time. The result of his reign as city
architect are the broad streets, the wide squares and half a score
of his splendid buildings which still remain as he planned them.
The most notable is the Town Hall, which Augsburgers claim
as the first 'skyscraper' in Europe.

The Rathaus is, of course, no skyscraper to us. Indeed, it
looks as wide as it is high, though its solidity is dissipated by
the two towers with their cupolas rising outside the central
gable. To the 16th-century Augsburgers, whose three- or four-
storey houses seemed higher than they really were because
they were so narrow, the seven-storey building must have
seemed colossal. Below the gable the imperial eagle still gleams
with gold.

I tried to imagine Elias Holl himself, with black doublet and
hose, silver-buckled shoes, short spade beard and curling
moustachios, pacing about the square, covered then with piles
of masonry and busy with workmen. I thought of him arguing
with his critics, pacifying the burghers, flinging out his hands
with the gestures he had learned in Italy – the land where, in
Venice and Milan, he had first had his dream of turning

Augsburg into the finest renaissance city in Europe.

Then, from his imaginings, I moved on into the 16th century itself.

A few hundred yards from Holl's great creation, the Rathaus, I walked through one of the four sets of gates, painted in diagonal brown and yellow stripes, which form the entrance to the Fuggerie. This strange, almost incredible, place is a link not so much with Holl as with his masters – the bankers who held the purse-strings of Europe in their hands.

The simplest description of the Fuggerie is that it is the oldest social settlement in Europe. The phrase does no justice to its calm serenity.

In the 14th century a village weaver named Hans Fugger settled in crowded Augsburg, and with him began one of the most extraordinary power-sagas of Europe. He flourished, and made his fortune, leaving it to be divided between his three sons. They, in turn, added to it. More significant, they used it to finance the great men of Augsburg. Others came to them from beyond the city, even beyond Bavaria. They became bankers to one after the other of the German states. Then to the Italian states. And, finally, to the ruler of the Holy Roman Empire himself. Their power and influence were more widespread and authoritative than those of the Rothschilds in a later age. The Fuggers were bankers to Europe.

Their home, the Fuggerhaus, was destroyed during the last war. The Fuggerie, however, is a better memorial to their compassion and piety than any patrician mansion could have been. It is because of this tiny 'city within a city' that their name is mentioned every day with reverence and gratitude instead of being merely another name in a history book.

As I walked into the little walled-in village it was so quiet that I felt an intruder. In mid-morning there were no other sightseers. A writer in the 17th century wrote a description of it which might equally well have been written today. The houses were each of two storeys, 'the lower one with a little court or garden, the upper one with a loft'. The gardens were not to be seen, for they are at the back of the houses. For the rest, they were the same.

The streets were wide enough for a cart. The walls of the houses were a deep, rich ochre, one of the Fugger colours which appear on the gates. Where the streets crossed a small fountain trickled with water, red geraniums round it.

The Fuggers, to whom every royal house in Europe was in debt, completed this tiny 'town' in 1525. There were 106 houses, built for burghers and workmen of good repute. These elderly citizens were, of course, all Catholics and a small church was built for them within the walls. A house and office were provided for the 'administrator'. The Fuggerie was an act of charity, in the truest and oldest meaning of that word, long before municipalities had any sense of 'social welfare' responsibility.

It remains as it was built. After the bombing and shelling of the last war, when a few of the houses were destroyed, they were restored with such exactness that it is impossible, now, to tell the difference. Every Sunday the little church is filled, and mass is said for the souls of its founders. Every day, too, each householder is committed to say an *Ave Maria* for the great bankers. They may do so with profound thanksgiving. When Ulric, Georg and Jakob Fugger went to see their first tenants they assured them that their rents would never go up. In 1525 the old burghers paid one mark seventy-five pfennigs a year. Incredibly, the promise has been kept. The tenants in the Fuggerie still pay no more than their 16th-century forbears. In English money it works out to about three shillings a year; in American currency, about forty cents. It is not surprising they say their *Ave Marias* with joy.

I looked round carefully, and took three photographs, but

when an old man came and stood in his doorway, I put my camera away as if I had been caught in some disreputable act. I still felt an intruder.

An hour later we drove out of Augsburg on the last lap of our journey to Oberammergau.

To me, Augsburg will always be the city of Elias Holl, of broad and splendid streets, of renaissance fountains . . . of the Fuggerie, and serenity a stone's throw from the centre of the town. I am still sorry that, for the rest of the family, it remains only 'that place where we couldn't get any coffee'.

9) *Village of the Vow*

'AND THAT'S where Hitler wrote *Mein Kampf!*'

We were on the by-pass that skirts the old town of Landsberg, still on the Romantic Road. To the left rose the citadel-fortress where Hitler had been imprisoned in 1924. 'And the Nazis who were waiting trial in Nurnberg after the war were imprisoned there, too,' I added. It seemed a kind of rough justice that those who carried out the conquest planned in *Mein Kampf* should end up where the dream began.

It was too good a day for political discussion, certainly about any Right Wing resurgence in the Germany of our time – though all at once we wondered what some of the friendly people we had met really thought about it, and about us, underneath their gracious charm. Nor had we time to explore Landsberg itself – this town where two Roman roads once crossed. One was the *Via Claudia*, linking Augsberg and Rome, and the other the 'salt road' from Bavaria to the west. In leaving Landsberg behind us we were saying farewell to the mediaevalism of Belgium, Luxembourg and Germany.

We were about to enter another world.

G

The last town we came to on the Romantic Road was Schongau, and the change was already evident.

We parked in a little square that was all lightness, and yet gentle to the eyes. At midday we had a café to ourselves and feasted on strawberry-cake and cream. Or almost to ourselves. The only other coffee-drinker was an elderly lady who took us for Americans and told us about her son who lived in the Y.M.C.A. in Michigan. We left her, happy in her thoughts – 'he is a good boy . . . he never forgets me' – and went to glance in the church. This was our first introduction, on this journey, to the baroque which would be with us through Austria and into Switzerland. Though there was less gilt, less cherubs and angels, less exuberant *décor* than in the sensuous devices of Bavaria and Austria, the extravagance took our breath away.

'You'll see better than this at Wies,' I promised, 'when we see the castles!'

How wrong I was!

From a hayfield, where we picnicked on fresh rolls, *Wurst* and cheese half an hour later, we had out first view of the Bavarian alps. The new landscape was of fields dotted with chalets and tiny barns. The small churches were onion-topped, and we could imagine the gaiety of the saints and ceilings. Two old men walking by us with wooden hayrakes gave us '*Gruss Gott*' as they passed, and we already sensed the independence of spirit, the deep love of the land, the simple piety and the open-heartedness of those we were going amongst.

A short while, and we drove into the small Bavarian village which half the western world comes to see. Oberammergau, 'the village of the vow', maintains its integrity to the cross set on the hill above the parish church, despite all the commercial pressures of tourism, radio, television and journalism. Those who stay here for a while, who get close to the heart of its people, know that it is round the church rather than the shops or even the theatre that its life really revolves.

I had been to Oberammergau on other occasions, though the most memorable was in 1960, when I was one of more than a million visitors to the Passion Play. But, apart from the Play, thousands of tourists fill its streets every year, buy its products, watch its woodcarvers at work and are taken round the theatre in carefully shepherded national groups. Streets and restaurants were crowded this July afternoon when we arrived, and there were more coaches and cars than we saw at any other place on our travels. North American accents predominated, but they were punctuated by the staccato of the Latins, the gutturals of Holland and Scandinavia and the sibilance of the Asians. Cameras clicked everywhere.

It is fashionable to dismiss Oberammergau as 'pretty', 'over-rated', 'commercialised' or 'self-conscious'. These are gross libels. I can think of no other village but Nazareth to which the Christian world turns its steps in such numbers – and Oberammergau is certainly more Christian than Nazareth, and possibly less spoiled. Of course, the touring companies have cashed in. So have photographers and the mass-media men. It would not be surprising if the villagers *were* commer-cialised or self-conscious. The miracle is that it remains so truly itself, so much the village under the cross, where it is a privilege to live, a deeper privilege to have been born.

This is so because the Passion Play is not 'done for visitors'. The village is glad to have them, and is grateful for the pros-perity they have brought. Yet any Oberammergauer would give the same answer as I was given by Anton Preisinger, who played the Christus in 1950 and 1960.

'What would you do now without your visitors?'

'We would not live so well. But we would still produce the Play whether anyone came to see it or not,' this gentle, dis-tinguished man replied. 'It is not played for the world, but for God.'

It was in Preisinger's hotel, the *Alte Post*, with its gilt post-

horn hanging outside, that we had tea. The interior is busy,
quiet and dark. Inevitably, a cluster of teaspoons hangs on the
wall, trophies of the shooting matches which the owner had
won. Outside, the chalet-frontages were brightened by murals
and window-boxes. But then, so is almost every house in the
place. Indeed, it is here that one first meets the custom of
painting every possible house-wall with designs which vary
from the sun or the eagle to some monstrous allegorical
picture.

Even in Oberammergau the murals are by no means
exclusively religious, though the most striking ones are linked
with the Passion theme. These were mostly painted by Franz
Zwink, an Oberammergau artist who worked between 1735
and 1788. The most notable are those on the wall of the
Pilatushaus, which from a distance transform the flat surfaces
into three-dimensional pillars, arcades, balconies and steps – the
Bavarian impression of a first-century Palestinian official
residence which ends up by being neither Roman nor German,
merely 18th century!

There is more to see in the village than the afternoon visitor
may realise, and the only sensible thing to do is to spend a
night here – or, if you are visiting the Play, to come back for a
day. It would be a pity, for instance, to miss the fairy-tale
murals of Red Riding Hood and Hansel and Gretel, with
wolves, witches and gingerbread houses brightening the outside of the two orphanage houses beyond the railway station.
Less garish and more detailed than most, they might have been
copied from a last-century German story book.

These two houses well illustrate the answer to a question
which all visitors ask.

'You must make a tremendous amount of money every ten
years!' The question implies the comment that everything,
including play-tickets, ought to be a great deal cheaper than it
is. 'What do you do with it all?'

I once asked this myself.

'There were times when the play cost a great deal more to put on than we ever got back.' The rest of the answer was more convincing. 'Our actors have to give up work not only for the period of the play but for many months previously for rehearsals. They have to be recompensed. The theatre itself takes a great deal of keeping up. There are costumes, musicians, attendants, guides, all sorts of staff. They all take money.'

'But you must make huge profits?'

'Selling tickets, and making bookings, is much too big a job to tackle ourselves. And the agents don't do it for nothing, I can assure you. They take their cut. But . . . yes, it is true. There *are* profits. But just as we do the Play to the glory of God, so we use the profits for the benefit of his people. And children. The children in the Hansel and Gretel houses are maintained by them. Orphanages, schools, old people's homes, churches all over the diocese are helped.' My informant spread his hands widely. 'It goes in helping others, *mein Herr*. I can assure you that we do not sit down when the Play is over and distribute it amongst ourselves.'

His last comment, as we parted, was realistic: 'The Play has brought more prosperity to us than our fathers ever knew. We are thankful we live when we do.'

Next to the Play, it is the woodcarvers who contribute most to the image of the village. Nowadays the Passion is dominant in their craft. But it is strange to think that, though they had been at work here since the 16th century, it was not until somewhere about 1880 that the Play itself provided a motif for their art. Before that, they concentrated on toys.

Lang is a common name in the village and one family of Langs greatly affected its life. Josef Lang settled here in 1736 as a craftsman. His skill passed from generation to generation until the last direct descendant, Guido Lang, founded the Lang Art and Culture Museum in a house specially built for the purpose. After his death in 1921 the municipality acquired both the building and its collection of folk-art which spanned four hundred years. I would be surprised if the visitor is not more intrigued by the toys than by anything else.

By the last century, woodwork was being exported all over Europe and America. But they export more than their products, for one of the pleasantest surprises in St Ives is to find an Oberammergau Lang making wood-carvings in the clear light of Cornwall.

Naturally we made our way to the church. Its interior seemed flooded with light, illuminating every rococo detail, flashing on the gilded cherubs, bursting back again from the intricate gold and white glory of the high altar. The Passion itself is imprinted deeply on the minds of the worshipping villagers for there is a stone *pietà* at the entrance – an old, worn, rather grotesque group of the Madonna holding her crucified son. Sitting in the gallery, its uncomfortable wooden benches worn smooth with the years, we looked below and could imagine the village gathering here to pray before the cast of the Play is chosen each tenth year. Here, too, every day of the performance, all the players come to offer themselves and their day's work as the priest celebrates Mass.

The church, rebuilt between 1736 and 1741 by Josef Schmutzer, stands on the site of the original one which was destroyed by fire. But until 1820 the Play was performed either in the church itself or the churchyard – a reminder that, until recently, it was very much a private devotion of the village itself.

I have written as if there were only one vow, but in fact Oberammergau owes its past existence and present prosperity not to one, but to two, vows. The first was an emperor's, the second its own.

In 1330 the Emperor Ludwig the Bavarian was returning from the wars in Italy, where he had vowed to build a monastery when he arrived once more on German soil. On his arm he carried a strange, miraculous image of the Virgin which he had seized from an Italian church. At the top of the pass above the hamlet of Oberammergau his horse suddenly dropped to its knees. He pulled it up sharply, but it knelt a second and a third time by a tall spruce tree. The emperor accepted its behaviour as a divine indication that this was the place for his monastery. Here, where it now stands in its sombre glory, the church and monastery of Ettal was built. The steep pass to Ettal, with Oberammergau at the bottom of the hill, became a newly-frequented trade route, and the village received un-usual privileges from the emperor. It was on these privileges and freedoms that its prosperity was first founded.

Even so, had it not been for the plague and Kaspar Schisler, the world would never have heard of it. The emperor's vow may be legend, but this is fact. In 1632 the plague, brought to the valleys by the Swedish mercenaries who later fought their way up the Romantic Road, ravaged the whole neighbour-hood. In parishes such as Bobing and Karlgrub all the inhabi-tants died or fled. Oberammergau put an embargo on anyone leaving or entering the village. It was poor Schisler, working nearby at Eschenlohe, who took the risk of imprisonment to see his family and made his way in by an unguarded path. He brought the Black Death with him. Family after family was wiped out.

In despair, the village council made its vow. If God would stop the plague they pledged themselves and their descendants to present the Passion of our Lord once every ten years. From that moment, the chronicler records, the plague claimed no more victims. Two things support the old tale. The first is the sudden cessation of deaths in the parish register.

The other is that the following year, 1634, the solemn promise was redeemed for the first time. The Passion Play of Oberammergau had begun.

From 1640, its ten-year cycle broken only by war in our own century, the vow has been kept. Religiously kept. It is the only appropriate phrase.

There were crowds of people in the *Spielhaus* – they prefer the word 'playhouse' to 'theatre', for no other play is ever presented here. In the huge auditorium, with its seats for 5,000 people, groups were being shown round by guides speaking German, French, Spanish, Italian and English. The playhouse itself is too familiar to need description, with its open view of the stage from every seat and its magnificent acoustics. The stage, of course, is open to the sky and, beyond it, the hills rise steep and green. But only when we stood on the stage itself did we realise its immensity. It was no longer surprising that a crowd-scene of five hundred or more can be marshalled here to clamour for Christ's death when Pilate appears at the top of the palace steps. What is much more surprising is the realisation that a group of woodcarvers, hoteliers, shop-keepers and the like, without any professional training and with no aids such as make-up or microphones, can hold a crowd of five thousand or more in silence, and often in reverence, for eight hours a day.

Behind the stage we were shown the dressing-rooms, the cross and the crown of thorns, the two sets of robes for each character, one for fine weather and one for rain. Both sets are needed most weeks. It is almost unbearable to see the Passion enacted while clouds gather on the hills, splitting with lightning flashes and thunder as the cross is raised. Such things happen here. Nature adds a violence to the Play such as the most adventurous producer could never devise.

Our night in the village was spent not in a hotel but in a *Haus* – an ordinary chalet, perhaps two hundred years old. It had no frescoes outside, but plenty of evidence inside of the craft most followed in the village. Our hostess's forbears would not have qualified for the present School of Wood-carvers, but must have found fulfilment in their own simple achievements. Our interest, however, was less in the house than in our host and hostess. Franz and Gudrun were youngish middle-aged villagers and, as we sat and talked in a room dominated by a decorative cuckoo-clock, we asked the questions they must get weary to death of answering. Yet, far from seeming bored, they appeared to light up from within when they talked of the one thing they loved above all others.

'You have been in the Play?' we asked.

'Of course. Almost everyone is, sometime or other. Only members of the crowd. A Roman soldier once. We are not actors like Preisinger and Schweigerhof.'

'There must be very few actors like Hans Schweigerhof,' I commented. His characterisation of Judas in 1960 brought him professional offers and unstinted praise from the world's press.

'It was better here in 1960 than in 1950. There was less commercialism. Fewer souvenir stands. Fewer people cashing in from outside,' Franz said.

His wife cut in, sharply. 'We don't like being exploited. Some of the old people say things would be better as they used to be, before the new theatre was built for the 1930 play.'

'People think we make a lot of money from the performances, but they forget how much goes to agencies outside the village. And how much had to be done after the war. The 1950 Play didn't nearly put things right. The village had been full of soldiers—'

'There was the Messerschmidt factory here, too,' added Gudrun.

'—and when it was over,' went on Franz, 'everything . . . houses . . . roads . . . waterworks . . . everything needed repair. In 1946 the costumes had not been attended to for sixteen years. You can imagine what that cost. Costumes for seven hundred people – two sets, in many cases.'

Gudrun, a true *Hausfrau*, leaned forward. 'And new shoes . . . for all the seven hundred in the cast!'

'Had you got the money to spend? Profits from the Plays before the war?'

They shook their heads. 'After all the money they spent when the new theatre was built for the 1930 performances? We had to borrow a million marks from the German Government.'

We asked about the play and the players – the things that interest everybody.

'Is it only the villagers who are allowed to appear in the Play?'

'What you call the "locals"? Yes,' replied Franz.

Gudrun smiled at her husband. '*He* wasn't born here, but he's allowed to join in because he had the good sense to marry *me*! A man may be a player if he marries an Oberammergau girl, you see. In five years he can be one of the crowd. Ten years for a speaking part.'

'We had an American boy in the crowd once because he had been born here. His parents had lived in the village since the war ended.'

'But mostly they're *real* villagers?' I saw Gudrun smile at her husband as we asked.

'Oh yes. Certainly. Some of the actors have ancestors whose names are recorded as taking part in the first Play. In 1633.'

'It's funny about the donkey, too,' Gudrun laughed. 'Until 1950, for generations, there had only been one donkey in the parish. So *his* ancestors took part, too.' She went on to describe how the donkey has to go and live with the 'Christus' for the rehearsals and the whole period of the Play.

We questioned them about the actors, for we had seen a TV programme about their being chosen, in the church itself.

'That's right. They're chosen by popular vote. They've got to be good men as well as good actors, you see. And all the

women must be . . . unmarried . . .' she hesitated to say
'virgins', '. . . even in the chorus.'

The cuckoo clock reminded us that our host and hostess
might want to go to bed, and we apologised for keeping them.
'We're used to questions,' Franz smiled. 'Even if most of the
answers are in the guide books.' It was too friendly for a
rebuke.

As we went for a last walk round the village, completely
quiet now, it was not hard to recapture some of my experi-
ences when I had seen the Play myself. I cannot forget the
moment after the chorus, a long line acting as a sort of human
curtain which reappeared between each of the scenes, dis-
persed at the beginning of the Play. Suddenly the stage was
filled with an excited crowd, and I was aware that, in the
middle of it, was a man on a donkey. At that moment we were
not in a Bavarian village at all. Christ had come to Jerusalem.
It was as natural as that.

More terrible was another crowd scene in the afternoon.
The previous day I had been sightseeing in the village when,
across the houses, came a shout, passionate and violent, ripping
into the calm tea-time air. We knew then only that it came
from the playhouse. Sitting in the auditorium I recognised it
again. It came from five hundred throats, its guttural hoarse-
ness as terrible as the cry of a Nazi rally roused by a Jew-
baiting *Gauleiter*. It was the '*Crucify! Crucify!*' that assailed
Pilate's judgement-seat in Jerusalem.

But the awful thing about it was the epidemic nature of it
all. I was so infected by the emotion of the crowd that I felt,
had I been in Jerusalem that day, I could not have escaped
shouting, too. It was thrust into my mind that in any moment
of political decision it is not easy to stand silent and alone,
much less protest.

One other personal reaction remains with me. People ask if
the Play is impressive. Of course it is. It stays with you for life.

It is something not to be missed, and it cannot be forgotten.
There is no difficulty in following it, for you have a trans-
lation in your own language as well as the German text. In
any case, it exactly follows the Gospel story from the entry
into Jerusalem. But, for me, it was real and compelling right
up to the raising of the cross and the dull sound as it dropped
into the hole. The hammering of the nails had sounded
unbearable. Yet, at that moment when there began the long
twenty minutes during which the 'Christus' hung before our
eyes, the reality of the Play – for me – turned to 'theatre'.
The flesh-coloured skin tights, the thrust spear and running
blood, were unreal as nothing, up till then, had been. I did not
lose interest – that would be impossible – but I suddenly lost
conviction.

Now the remarkable thing was that that was the moment
when it seemed to come to life for many of those sitting
round me. Not the British and American tourists, but the
Germans and Austrians, the Italians and the Spaniards. I saw
the tears in their eyes and on their faces. Momentarily, I
wondered why. And then I remembered the *pietà* in the
church porch . . . the wayside shrines, with a bunch of fresh
flowers placed by a passing peasant as he went to his morning
work. I realised that these people, too, had been to Mass that
day, like the actors themselves. They had seen the elevation of
the Host – the word that comes from the Latin *hostes*, which
means the victim, the sacrifice.

Thinking so, I understood two things more clearly. One
was why my neighbours were so moved. This was a visual
enactment of daily worship. The other was why Anton
Preisinger had said: 'If not one came to see it we would still
present our Play. We do not do it for the world, but for the
glory of God.'

10) *Below the Zugspitze*

ON THE road from Oberammergau to the Tyrol two miles of 'no man's land' separates Germany from Austria. We were waved into it at the one frontier and out at the other with little fuss and no problems. It is an area of thick woodland, without any house or cottage, and no one lives there.

We had made only two short stops on the way. The first was at Ettal, to look at the domed monastery built where the Emperor's horse bowed by the spruce-tree, and where the monastic liqueurs on sale ranged from baby-size to pint-size bottles. It is a trade endemic to religious houses, apparently. The second was at the twin town of Garmisch-Partenkirchen. Despite its old houses it somehow always leaves an Edwardian impression on me. The most popular winter-sports centre in Germany, it is exorbitantly expensive compared with most of Austria. Watching a group of self-conscious American tourists riding by in a *barouche*, obviously enjoying themselves, and sauntering round the tree-shaded streets, I felt slightly guilty that I liked the place so little. In the winter, when roofs, fields and mountains are covered with snow, it is no doubt quite different. It is even more expensive!

Beyond the frontier, Lermoos was a little huddle of houses
round the church across the valley. A signpost marked the
road to Ehrwald, a road that goes nowhere else and climbs
gently towards the mountains. On one side the massive,
barren, grey Zugspitze rose above us, its summit lost, as it
often is, in the clouds. On the opposite side, the cone-shaped
Sonnenspitze was flanked by lower peaks. In between lay the
green valley of Ehrwald.

'Isn't it *lovely*!'

An uncountable number of visitors must have said the same
thing. And so it is. Not so long ago a desperately poor hamlet,
it has become one of the Tyrol's most delightful holiday
centres. We were glad we had decided to stay three nights
here, to soothe our travel-taut nerves. Then, recalling the
moment when I had looked up the 'Fodor' *Austria* at home,
I stopped the car and pointed up the Zugspitze. Half way up
the mountain-side, now just below the cloud-base, the funicular had stopped. A tiny building was visible beyond it.

'That's the place,' I said.

'What place?'

'The *Alpenhotel Zugspitzbahnhof*!'

Light dawned, abruptly. 'The mountain hotel? The place
you nearly booked us in at?' They stared at it incredulously,
and then turned on me, all three of them. 'If we'd landed up
there your life wouldn't have been worth living!' How well I
knew it.

Even so, we were not staying at the hotel I had tried to
reserve. Instead, a letter had come back from the Tourist
Office. '*The hotel you have chosen is closed in case of death*'. In
case of whose death they did not specify. Instead, they had
transferred us to the *Sonnenspitze*, a tall, gabled, white and
welcoming building just on the edge of the village green. As
good as you could find in the village. For excellent food and
drink, splendid accommodation and the friendliest possible

service, we paid a very modest sum indeed. Already, before we had opened the car door, the welcome was apparent. A dark young man was opening the door, and introduced himself as Mohamed.

'I am Moroccan,' he introduced himself, 'and my name is Pierre.' Later, he told us some of his adventures, working in garages and motor-manufacturers in Germany and Scandinavia preparatory to going home to take control of his father's business in Morocco. 'Working here will help. Tourists will be coming soon to Morocco as they do now to Spain.' When we asked how many languages he spoke he was a little vague. 'Arabic, French and English, of course. Naturally some Spanish. I had to learn German for the factory work, and then a bit of Swedish.' It was nothing to boast about, it seemed.

Our bedroom windows looked out to the Zugspitze and down across the valley, and the view that first evening was superb. The clouds had, for once, lifted from the summit and, while the valley lay in a golden haze, the grey mountain-side changed slowly from pink to bronze, bronze to gold, capped by flashing snow.

If there is little to do in Ehrwald, that is its special charm. A café or two, a few shops, a 'folk evening' at the hotel once a week and songs led by a zither in the *Weinkeller*, . . . a chair-lift . . . and a profusion of walks. The green, unusual in its size, with red seats dotted here and there, is almost like a village cricket green in Surrey or Sussex. There were brown cows cropping across it, grazing on the sweet grass by the tiny, unused, square chapel at the farther end, as we walked across it.

Many visitors with a day to spare go by the mountain-railways to the summit of the Zugspitze, and it is worth the journey. Instead, we chose to spend the afternoon on the chairlift and the Alm. We walked past the 'Peppermill', saw Ehrwald's waterfall – at this time of high summer no more than a thin trickle dropping down the face of the cliff – paused to look at the ski-jump, and then swung upwards alongside the grim, shaley wall of the Zugspitze to the top of the Alm. The chair-lift was a new amenity since I had last been in the village, and a very considerable asset in reaching the lovely walking-paths in the upper valley.

To get into the chairs we had to stand with our back to them as they came round, and then step up and drop into the seat as the chair swung on its way. Leaping out at the top was easier.

Susan was intrigued. 'Doesn't anyone ever get stuck?' In reply I told the story of the large, cumbrous lady in a party I once took up a Swiss mountain. Getting on was not too difficult, though she had to be pushed. Then she just fell into the chair, and cheerfully waved goodbye. But, while other people got off at the top, she still had her safety-bar across her ample self – and came on down again. That would not have been so bad if she had managed to get off at the bottom. Unhappily, though she had now got the bar undone, she herself was firmly wedged. To the hilarious delight of the rest of the party and the astonishment of the lift-man she was off again up the mountain-side, waving just as cheerfully and asking us to wait until she managed to come down and stay down.

Below the swinging chairs the meadows had been carpeted with flowers and it was impossible to walk anywhere without crushing them. Walking paths, going in a dozen different directions, were marked in hours instead of miles. But the marking is deceptive. It applies to local people who are accustomed to hill-climbing and not to soft-muscled British tourists. We found no edelweiss but there was an astonishing profusion of other blossoms. Little brilliant patches of blue took us to the gentian. Tiny field-anemones were everywhere. And, higher still, dark red clusters under the trees and on the banks were alpenroses. When we counted them out in our hotel room we had gathered forty-nine varieties – and we must have missed as many as we picked.

On our way back to the hotel we went into the church, whose outer wall is painted with a modern, psychedelic fresco. Inside there was none of the customary baroque. Instead, its walls and ceilings were painted, in the same garish colours, with angular red and blue angels surrounding a sort of 'Tate Gallery' Creator and Madonna. In the hotel we later asked Herr Leitner, our amiable host, how the villagers like it. We were not surprised when he was non-commital. Then we asked about the tiny church on the green, whether it were ever used.

'Very occasionally,' he told us. 'But, of course, it used to be the only church there was. That one,' he waved towards the staring mural, 'is comparatively new.' Then, seeming to change the subject, he asked us if we liked the village, if we thought it clean and tidy. Before we could do more than nod he went on.

'It wasn't always like this, you know. All this part of the village is new. The hotels and the shops came with the tourists. Until the vogue for winter sports this was a terrible place. Terrible. Other mountain villages were much the same, off the beaten track, like Ehrwald. The people could hardly make a bare living from the soil. Over there' – he indicated the open valley towards Lermoos – 'it was different. There were good fields in the valley. But up in the mountains – nothing. Just a few shacks . . . chalets that were almost falling down . . . two families to a house; a thing unheard of . . . dreadful poverty. You can see the size of the old village by the size of the tiny chapel on the green. There wasn't even a priest.

'Then the tourists started to come for the winter sports. Everything was changed. It's not surprising we're friendly, and try to make you feel at home. You've brought life to our people.'

H

Britain, unfortunately, was bringing little life to Ehrwald that summer. Apart from a couple of coachloads of transients, we were the sole Britishers in the hotel in a fortnight, Herr Leitner confessed.

'What about these castles we're going to see?' my wife asked, next morning.

'Linderhof and Neuschwanstein.'

'And the church. What's it called?'

'Wies. Yes. We'll go this afternoon. I've got to go to the bank and change a cheque this morning.'

For once, everyone was ready on time, and we drove out across the valley, through Lermoos. The Austrian customs-post stood in the shadow of the trees, a few miles beyond Reutte. The officer came out, swung back the gate, and waved us through.

'No trouble, these customs men. They just don't bother.'

The German officer stepped forward half a mile farther on, asking us where we were going before he opened the gate to let us through. He was enthusiastic about the Bavarian king's castles, and pencilled out a more interesting route than the one I had planned to use.

'Your passports, please.'

Then, catastrophically, I remembered. Coming back from the bank I had left them – for the only time – on the dressing table. All of them.

The officer was as distressed as we were. We *ought* to see the castles. Passports – everybody has a passport anyway. He swallowed hard on his regulations. 'Perhaps we could forget them. Just your *grüne Karte*, then.'

That was the end. The 'green card', sign of an international motor-car insurance, was with the passports. No one can be allowed on the road without his green card. The German officer regretted deeply, but. . . .

We turned the car and drove back into Austria. Or almost into Austria. The policeman at the Austrian barrier, who had been so negligent ten minutes before, held up his hand authoritatively.

'Passports?'

I tried to explain.

'Green card?' He held out his hand and, in return, I held mine out, empty.

He started to shout, using words I had never heard before. He *must* have our passports, the green card. I felt cold pimples forming all over me. We could not get into Germany. Nor could we get back into Austria. We were firmly established in 'no man's land', and the officer was not inclined to relent. Unlike the 'no man's land' between Ehrwald and Oberammergau, where no one lives, this stretch seemed likely to have four people and a car in it for a long, long time.

Suddenly he shouted even louder and pointed to the white house inscribed *Zoll . . . Polizei*. I followed him in and tried to follow his explanation. The man at the table was obviously *dolizei* rather than *zoll*.

'You have a wife? In the car? I will permit her to go and get the passports and the card. Even though it is against the regulations.'

'In the car?'

That set him off again, even louder than his subordinate. Then, all at once, he became more gentle – as gentle as a bull in the ring that waits for breath to charge again. 'We will forget the passports. It is the green card that is important. You cannot drive without insurance.' He considered, silently. 'I *could* give you a card that would permit you to drive for twenty-four hours.'

I pointed out that I only wanted to drive for half an hour, to Ehrwald. He bent across his desk and took up a form. 'We keep these for emergencies like this. It will cost you thirty schillings.'

It was only when I had paid up and got the form in my hand that I realised he had a pile of forms – for emergencies – some four inches high.

The family never saw the castles, after all. It was a great pity, for they are very much worth seeing.

They owe their existence to a king who may have been mad, whose memory the country-people still keep gloriously alive, who was deposed by the Bavarian Government for his reckless extravagances – and from whose fantastic castles the government has been reaping a harvest of tourists' Deutschmarks which surely must have repaid the exchequer many times over.

But *was* Ludwig II of Bavaria mad? It is very hard to say.

Born in 1845 – he died in 1886 – he was the son of Maximilian II. His father built the castle of Hohenschwangau, a marvellous re-creation of mediaeval baronial splendour, and it was there that Ludwig grew up in an atmosphere of almost limitless and easily squandered wealth. Idealistic, with effeminate good looks, and introspective, two things conditioned his day-dreams. One was the first time he heard Wagner's *Lohengrin*. He nearly fainted with ecstasy at the music. The other was the legendary *Schwangau* – the swan which gave its name to the district and to the castle. He associated it, mystically, with Lohengrin's swan, and it seems that, as time went by, he fancied himself to be a new Lohengrin – a dangerous dream for an immature, lonely boy. But, for Ludwig, there was no Elsa. There should have been, for he married his beautiful cousin, Elizabeth – but the marriage was a failure. He never lived with his wife.

In 1864 he succeeded his father as King. He was a shrewd ruler and there is nothing in his political activities to suggest that he was unbalanced.

And yet . . . to visit Linderhof. . . .

Not far from Ettal and Oberammergau the Linderhof castle

stands in the midst of the woods. Across an ornamental lake, where an immense fountain rises from a group of figures covered with gold-plate, stands an 18th-century French chateau, perfect in every architectural detail.

The linden tree is still there, just by the fountain, a giant tree that gave its name to the family which farmed the land here for centuries as tenants of the Ettal monks. Maximilian used the farm as a hunting lodge. Ludwig had it pulled down, and re-erected nearby, so that he could build the chateau. Inside, the castle is incredible with its gold and gilt, its painted ceilings, its Versailles-like mirrors that extend the small rooms in an infinite distance of reflections. Here Louis of the Revolution and his Marie Antoinette might easily have loved and lived. But the sybaritic Ludwig, it seems, loved no one but himself. The ornate golden bed looks down on a long vista of Italianate waterfalls – and it is a bed for one. The marble dining-table, small and on a movable platform, would descend through the floor to be replenished because the King would not have menials about him as he ate.

In the garden is a Moorish kiosk, bought from the Paris Exhibition. And there the lonely King sat and smoked his hookah.

More astonishing still is the concrete grotto, with a 'subterranean lake' where a swan rides at anchor, while beyond the lake is a stage specially created for a performance of *Lohengrin*. Echoes made it impossible to sing in the confined space. That, however, did not trouble the composer. The important thing was that, because of the King's patronage and wealth, Wagner was able to continue his work.

The Linderhof chateau was not the first of Ludwig's building fantasies. He had already begun to build a palace at Neuschwanstein – the 'swan' motif is in evidence again – before the architect was called away to design Linderhof. Completed after Linderhof, Neuschwanstein is probably the most incredible castle in Germany. Incredible because it is perched high on the hills overlooking the Alpsee and is itself such a collection of turrets, towers and pinnacles that one forgets its massive walls and thinks of it, instead, as ethereal. Inside the castle are huge rooms – notably the Hall of Singers decorated with scenes from *Parsifal*. Yet Ludwig, who regarded this as a 'castle of the Holy Grail' spent only four months of his life here.

Before it was completed he had already decided that it was not sufficiently isolated for his moody solitariness and he began the construction of the lonely castle of the Herrenschiemsee. There, he had spent only twenty-three days when, in 1886, he was deposed by his government as unfit to rule. Imprisoned in the castle of Starnberg he was drowned in its lake the same year. How, nobody knows – or ever told.

It is no surprise that visitors are more intrigued by the man himself than by the fantasies in stone which he created. They ask questions no one can answer and perhaps, for a long time, no one ever will. Mark Gibbon, in an impressive book on *Western Germany*, tells of discussing with an Austrian author a project to write Ludwig's life-story. The count who had contemplated it remarked that, having read the king's diaries, he was convinced that he was less a case for a biographer than for a psychologist – presumably one who dealt with abnormal psychology. It is easy to make guesses but, perhaps, unprofitable.

Those who visit Neuschwanstein will certainly not want to miss the 'pilgrimage church in the meadow' at Wies. The last creation of the Bavarian architect, Domenicus Zimmermann, and his brother, the painter and stucco-master, Johann Baptist Zimmermann, it is the most splendid baroque church in Germany. Here light is not merely something that comes through the unstained windows but is an almost physical part of the church itself. With an abandoned glorification of the senses in its gilt and gold, and its convoluted pillars which lead the eye to the richness of the ceiling, it manages, as someone has said, to put us in mind of heaven while unfailingly reminding us of the delights of earth.

Our disappointment at missing the castles was somewhat balanced by the evening in the hotel. One of the normal *Schuhplattler* nights, it had a rumbustious gaiety quite unusual and uninhibited. The audience was almost all German and Austrian. The orchestra went wild and the folk-dancers were thrust into stamping rhythms by German drinking songs as *Steins* thumped on the tables. For our own family the high-spot of the evening came when I was relentlessly dragged from the table by a girl in all her traditional finery and swung into a complex dance which left me completely breathless and all tangled up in knots. And left my wife and Susan in near-hysterics. I am no dancer, least of all a *Schuhplattler* dancer, but it was an experience to last for a long time.

Apparently it had not been forgotten by the gay Greta, either. She sailed down through the village on a Lambretta next morning as we were packing up the car and waved a laughing farewell. I was surprised the memory did not make her fall off her machine.

Postage-stamp Principality

'Got your passports?'

The question was obviously relevant but I decided to ignore it as we drove out of Ehrwald. The Zugspitze was veiling its majesty in cloud once more while, by contrast, the Sonnen-spitze's tall cone was bathed in sunlight. Across the valley, in Lermoos, they call it the Mittagspitze, because at noon the sun stands right above it in high summer. Now, our restful days over, we were once more on the run – to St Gallen, Lucerne and then five long days in the Oberland.

'Won't it be lovely to see the blue lakes again?' said my wife, nostalgically. And added: 'If they *are* blue!'

Our first lake was a deep green, and was still in Austria. After coming over the Fern Pass you see a turreted white castle, the Schloss Fernstein. The road swings at a right angle over a bridge and below you is a tiny lake, its green water made greener still by the trees that surround it. Two miniature islands turn it from a green pool into a picture. This is the Fern Lake, endlessly photographed, inadequately as a rule because the shadows and the coach's too brief stop make it hard to find a good angle.

From the Schloss the road winds on down the Fern Pass to join the 'A1' of continental Europe – the route which runs from the English Channel to the Black Sea. At Imst you could diverge completely from our own route and enjoy every moment of your journey. On a subsequent trip we have gone eastwards through Innsbruck, with its arcades, its royal palace and the Golden Roof, through the Eastern Tyrol to Salzburg. On a previous occasion I had taken a conducted party south from Innsbruck, through the Dolomites, into Italy. Make your own choice. Whatever it is you will be well rewarded. Ours was to turn our backs on Innsbruck, and drive westward to Switzerland and France.

We followed the Inn past a rock crowned with a castle in the middle of the valley. Here lived the real 'big bad wolf' – a baron named Wolff who terrorised the Austrian countryside in the same way as the barons of the Neckar valley. Farther on, Landeck is spoiled by the smoke and stench from the concrete factory, and my pleasantest memory is of a boy with a gentle fox-cub in his arms at the petrol station. It is a reasonably attractive road from here onwards through Vorarlberg, at any rate the first time or two you use it. The trouble is that, if you are staying in a place such as St Anton, you have to use it constantly to reach the eastern beauty spots and the passes into Italy.

We stopped for a moment. They were repairing the road – at its most picturesque point! The Trisanna valley leads southwards into the mountains, and the Trisanna bridge spans it like a slender thread. Below is the river and beyond the old Wiesberg castle. A train, bound towards Vienna, crawled slowly across the ravine, seemingly hesitant on the old viaduct. Soon afterwards the St Anton valley spread openly before us. The spire of St Jakob rose from the cluster of houses on our right, a baroque church whose gilded angels and flamboyant altar-piece contrast violently with the jostle of tumbledown cottages which surrounds it. The peak of the Valuga rose ahead of us and we were in St Anton.

St Anton is a long street of hotels, shops, *Gasthofs* and *Fremdenzimmer* chalets, pleasantly Tyrolean, but busy with a procession of traffic late into the night. It is, of course, a famous winter-sports centre and the 'Post' hotel displays a snobbery of photographs featuring stage, royalty and heaven knows who else to be found on St Anton's nursery slopes and ski-runs. But I have memories of a previous visit, which will last longer than those, or of listening to the village band, whose charming drum-majors were armed with little barrels of schnapps, or of tramping the snow-clad slopes of the Valuga.

Across the icy-cold Rosanna river a path leads through the trees to the upper end of the village. Part way up this path is a high wall enclosing the cemetery. Every grave has its wrought-iron cross, with the little mounted photographs of the dead, which look bizarre to a British visitor. At one end of the grave-yard is a chapel, with a modernistic sculpture, whose walls are covered, on one side, with place-names like Italy, France, Tobruk. On the other are the names of villagers who died in the last war. Amongst the battlefronts in this war memorial was an oddity. One painted scroll bore the abbreviation 'U.S.A.'

Back in the hotel I had asked Hans, the porter, to explain. His story went back to the days of the *Anschluss* when Austria was 'taken over' by the Nazis – a story now become vivid to a new generation through *The Sound of Music*.

'We in the villages had no love for the Nazis,' Hans explained, 'but it was not easy to escape. The frontiers were closely watched. Then Hans Schneider, one of our great skiers, gathered a band of men together. They were all used to the mountains, for in the winter we live on skis.'

'They managed to escape?'

'Yes. All of them. The man whose name is in the chapel

went to America. Some of the others did, too. But he joined the American Navy when the United States came into the war against Germany.'

'And against Austria, too.'

Hans nodded, 'He was killed at sea.' After a pause he went on. 'But he belonged to us, whoever he fought for.'

This time we did not climb up the path by the Rosanna but stopped at the little Café Sailer at the top of the village for coffee. We found a grim-faced Yorkshirewoman sitting by herself.

'I suppose you 'aven't seen a little man in a cap?'

We had not.

'I've lost him.' But there were no tears in her eyes.

'We'll send him back if we see him,' we promised as we left.

She looked at us coolly. 'You needn't bother!'

From St Anton the road climbs over the Arlberg pass, through the village of St Christoph with a memorial to the Free French forces – a stone cross of Lorraine. This pass is a good road with a few swinging hair-pin bends. To the north one sees one which is more exciting – the Flexen pass crawling down the mountain side, large stretches of its twisting length covered by a thick roof to protect traffic from avalanches and loose rocks. The Flexen leads to the lovely village of Lech, with a gay welcome for visitors. They have no chance to become more than visitors. The municipality has passed a law that property may never be sold to anyone but the families of the village itself.

Beyond the Arlberg, as you drop towards the plains, is a village with a reputation to rival Gotham. An Austrian friend told me about it.

'They used to make cheese here,' he said, 'and take it down to Feldkirch and Bludenz to sell in the market. Then some of the neighbouring villages started copying the Swiss – selling Gruyère cheese. You know, the sort with holes in it. After a while these villagers found there was no market for their cheese at all.

'So what did they do?' I had to ask the question.

'They held a meeting of the municipality and ended up by sending the mayor to Switzerland to buy a barrelful of holes!'

Because we wanted to stop in Liechtenstein as well as Pestalozzi we passed through Feldkirch and Bludenz without stopping. A pity, really; both are worth an hour or so. Then, down in the plains that seperate Austria and Switzerland, we edged along the Austrian frontier, following three coaches, and almost before we knew it were in Vaduz, the capital of Liechtenstein.

Indeed, it is the only bit of Liechtenstein that matters.

It is a real enough country, almost the smallest in Europe, with its own ruler and parliament. But its roots run far less deeply into history than Luxembourg'.

Until 1712 it did not exist. Its sixty-two square miles of mountains and valleys, with the strip of flat land by the river, were owned feudally by the lords of Vaduz and Schellenberg. Both paid allegiance to the Austrian Emperor. Then, in 1712, it was bought from the Emperor by an Austrian nobleman. Why, is uncertain. It did not appear to have any value. He can hardly have liked the look of it, for he had never seen it. Nor did he ever see it before his death in 1719. His son, Anton-Florian, had his 'lordship' raised by the Emperor Charles VI of Austria to a 'principality'.

But he never saw it either. Indeed, for a century after Anton-Florian's death, none of its rulers visited it. Then, in 1806, the Austrian empire collapsed and Liechtenstein's ruler was permitted by the 'powers' to become a Prince in his own right. Even that did not bring the ruler to his princedom. Not until 1842 did the Principality ever see its ruler, when Alois II of

Liechtenstein came to visit it. He must have liked it. He came twice before he died.

It was his successor who made sense of the situation. Johann II not only visited it: he lived there, in the castle high above Vaduz. More, he lived there throughout his long reign of seventy years. His power was absolute, but he chose to share it with his people. So things remained until 1921 when a new constitution was drawn up. The Prince retains his veto over legislation but the people, too, have their own power of veto. If four hundred men disapprove of a law they may demand a plebiscite. But only men. As in Switzerland, women have no vote.

Perhaps Anton-Florian and his successors need not be blamed for keeping away. The country is seven miles long, backed by mountains, and contains nothing that cannot be matched and bettered in Austria – except for the castle on the crag. Indeed, the main attraction for those who came before the last war was that nobody else came to it! 'Undiscovered' was a just word for it. Greta Gulbrannsen, a Scandinavian poet who lived in Liechtenstein, described it as 'a green island, untouched by time's stream'.

It is 'untouched' no longer. The coach companies discovered that by stopping at Lake Constance for lunch and at Vaduz for tea they could advertise a 'Four-Countries Tour', whether they started from Austria or Switzerland. That was the end of Gulbranssen's 'island of peace'. Few people stay there; thousands visit it each week.

Two things make it worth visiting, and at a third there is always a queue.

The first is the castle, for it transforms this little valley into something out of a fairy story. It stands high on the cliffs above Vaduz. With its pointed roofs there is something exquisite about it, whether against the blue skies of summer or the winter snow. The Prince's designation is the *Fuerst*. It is little wonder he is addressed as *Altesse Serenissime*, for his 'Serene Highness' is able to look down on everything he owns except the mountains. Though, if you climb a little way from the road which leads to the castle, you can even look down on the castle!

The queue of tea-time visitors at the post office is supporting Liechtenstein's chief industry. It is a philatelist's paradise. How many 'special issues' have been produced and superseded Stanley Gibbon's catalogue will tell you. For so small a state it must be rivalled only by Monaco. But there are other sources of income, too. Like the Bahamas, Liechtenstein offers considerable facilities to companies – some as short-lived as the 'special issue' stamps – who wish for a headquarters and a quiet but profitable life.

The other memorable place is seldom visited, and probably little-known. Beyond the Victorian, mock-gothic parish church is a solid, rectangular building with the date '1903' above the door. This unimaginative structure is the centre of Liechtenstein's legislative life.

'Is it really all right to go in?'

Inside, however, there was no one to stop us. The ground floor is the police headquarters, and the basement the state prison. The few policemen who sit here are the sole defence of the state (apart from the highly complex system of trenches, dug-outs and tank-traps between Vaduz and Switzerland) for its army was disbanded in 1868. By 1930 only one ancient soldier still remained – and you can buy his portrait in the picture-postcard shops.

We walked upstairs and looked round. Each door had a name on it. One seemed to belong to the Prime Minister. I knocked on it hopefully, and a neatly-dressed man looked out. He seemed surprised to see us.

'May we see the *Landtag*?'

He nodded. 'Certainly. We will be delighted.' His hand

was still on the door-handle. 'You know where it is? The next floor. You will perhaps excuse me if I do not come with you?' With a brief smile he went in and closed the door. Perhaps he was not the Prime Minister after all.

We opened a door on the top landing. Inside was a room no bigger than a mayor's parlour in a small town. The Prince's throne, of good, plain wood, stood below a portrait of the great ruler, Johann II. It was flanked by two other chairs and there was room, perhaps, for a score of men in the seats on the other three sides of the square. Two desks stood below the prince's dais. The walls were enlivened by portraits. No doubt some were of the Prince's remote ancestors who had never seen the land they ruled.

This was the *Landtag*, unfussy and efficient-looking, quietly distinguished. The smallest Parliament House in one of the smallest states in Europe. We were not tempted to risk a night in the basement cells by sitting in the *Serenissime*'s throne. Restrained in spirit, we made our way downstairs. No one took any more notice of our going out than they had of our coming in.

12) *Kindersymphonie*

'THEY LOOK exactly like the toy farm we had when we were children!'

No comment could have been more apt. True, we had reached Switzerland, but it had none of the familiar 'Alpine Calendar' features. They were to come later – but this was Appenzell. The psalmist would have felt at home here. The valleys were covered with corn and the hills with flocks – though the flocks were cattle, not sheep and goats. It is a pastoral land, thick with orchards, the green slopes of the hills dotted with farms. With bright red roofs, white walls, set in brilliant green fields studded with brown cattle and rounded trees, everything looked smaller than life – the very model for a child's toy farm. Yet, in fact, the high mountains are very close, and industrial Switzerland is a belt of busy towns just beyond the green hills. Perhaps because the modern world is so near Appenzell holds tenaciously to its traditional way of life – its cottage industries, its close-knit clans and families, its unchanged costume, its annual town and village *Landtags* and elections held in the open air.

Oberammergau: Alte Post Hotel

Oberammergau: Players arrive at the theatre

The Zugspitze, from Ehrwald

The Sonnenspitze, from Lermoos

When we drove into Trogen in the late afternoon we thought it was dead, though it was probably only the contrast with busy, gay Austria that gave the stolid, respectable buildings their sombre atmosphere of gloom. We were happy to leave it and, a little way out, drive through a field where a woman was pitching hay – the heavy work – to her husband on top of a cart. The scent of it pervaded the still, warm air and the Swiss flag at the end of the field-path hardly stirred in the breeze.

Children's voices rose sharply amongst the chalets by the flagpole. A young English voice called 'Hello' over the hedge. On a toddler's 'climber' a small girl with blonde hair worked energetically over and through the bars. Down the steps of a new chalet a group of almond-eyed children followed a man with a shaven head and long brown robes – a monk from Tibet. We saw the name outside one of the chalets. *Kindersymphonie*. The Children's Symphony.

We had arrived at Pestalozzi. Until a new village was built round an old manor house at Sedlescombe, near Hastings, a year or so ago, it was the only international children's village in Europe.

I first saw Pestalozzi in 1948, when there were seven new Appenzeller chalets grouped round an old farmhouse, whose barn provided a community centre which smelled of stored apples and hay. Since then it has grown in size, reputation and influence. Hundreds of children have passed through the houses and left the village, proud bearers of its 'Certificate of Citizenship'. All over Europe, and beyond it, 'friends of Pestalozzi' wear the little red ladybird that is its symbol.

But how did it all begin?

In the 1940s a young doctor, Walter Robert Corti, came to the end of his career. The son of a scientist from Ticino, the Italian-speaking part of Switzerland, he had qualified highly in

I

medicine and intended to become a specialist in brain-research. Then came tragedy. He developed tuberculosis. Instead of starting his career, he found himself at Davos, in the T.B. sanatorium.

Europe was at war, and Switzerland's neighbours were devastated both by bombing and by Nazi tyranny. The Jewish population had been decimated. But everywhere it was the children who were suffering most. Orphaned, homeless, starving, twisted in mind by the horrors of war, it was estimated soon after the war ended that there were 13,000,000 war orphans in Europe. To Dr Corti the total did not matter, but the plight of each single child mattered very deeply. He recalled how a young Swiss, Henri Dunant, had begun the Red Cross a century before, after seeing the tragic aftermath of Solferino. Should not Switzerland again take the lead in caring for those who suffered? True, over 200,000 children had been taken into Swiss homes for brief periods from its war-torn neighbours. But more than casual charity was needed.

In 1944 Dr Corti contributed an article to the weekly magazine, *Du*, in which he suggested that his country might become the site of an international children's village, on a sound educational basis, for a limited number of war orphans, in which they might learn the secret of living together. To his astonishment, the article produced not only a mass of correspondence but considerable offers of help.

As if in confirmation of his dream, he was pronounced symptom-free and discharged from the sanatorium the same year. He at once began to put his plan into action.

Offers of land came from all over the country and the farmhouse and land at Trogen was chosen. It was high enough for the air to be at its best but would suit children from the plains. Catholics and Protestants lived in amity together. There were evident openings in local industry for training. When I first visited the old farmhouse, and looked across the waters of the Bodensee, which we call Lake Constance, to Germany on the opposite shore and the hazy mountains of Austria to the south, it was clear that its geographical situation was ideal.

Corti's plan set the country's heart on fire. The first four houses were 'built' from money raised by the sale of 'ladybird badges'. Then they were 'sold' again. For £1,000 each they were 'bought' by the cities of Winterthur, Zurich and Basle and by CIBA, the chemical company, who handed them back again to the village. Migros, the Swiss commercial firm, gave the money for another, and so did a Masonic lodge, the 'Alpina'.

But, though they were paid for, bought and given back, they still had to be built! The layout of the village was planned and the chalets designed by the famous architect, Hans Fischli, as his gift to the children. Currency restrictions prevented money being sent in, so gifts in kind came instead. Coal from Poland, honey from Australia, oranges from Israel to be sold as national contributions. Swiss children took up an idea of Dr Corti's. All over the country they asked their municipality for a forest tree. With the help of the men it was cut down and sawn up. The children cut it into firewood and sold it to ready buyers. Altogether, the 'tree scheme' raised more than £15,000.

Then came the builders – volunteers from everywhere. German youths crossed the frontier to help. Art students came from Italy and France. Soldiers, demobilised or on leave, joined them. School-teachers paid their own fares from America. Altogether six hundred volunteers from seventeen nations – the largest contingent from Britain – put in 25,000 hours of labour.

The first orphans, selected by their own countries, were waiting, some in nearby Winterthur, for the completion of the houses. In 1946 the first chalet was completed and the French children moved in. Then came the Poles, later recalled by their own government. In 1947 there were three more houses, for the Austrians, Hungarians (also to be recalled), and Germans. In 1948 came the Italians, Finns and Greeks. The first houses for British children were occupied in 1950.

Today war orphans have given place to 'social orphans', 'half orphans' and refugees. The acceptance age has been raised. But Corti's original conception still holds good. 'National families living in an international community' remains the village pattern.

Our guide round the village was a Swiss girl and she was bombarded with questions which she answered in four languages. All the chalets are large, on the Appenzell pattern, with walls that give a Walt Disney impression of sloping outwards. Though the design is careful and integrated, the village is scattered about a compact area of the hillside much as a natural one would have been. One building that I remembered, however, was missing.

'What has happened to the farmhouse and the old barn?'

'We had to pull it down. A pity, really – but it was too old to stand up to two hundred children.'

'Are there two hundred here?' asked someone.

'Two hundred and thirty. From ten countries. All European except the Tibetan refugees.' She turned to the questioner. 'The Grand Lama of Tibet is our most distinguished patron.'

'How many houses are there?'

'Fifteen. The other community houses bring us up to twenty. Two each for the French, Greek, Italian and Tibetan children. One each for Austria, Germany, Finland, Great Britain and Switzerland.'

'But why *Swiss* children?'

'For the same reason they have British children at Sedlescombe. We want to share our traditions, and learn other people's. But, apart from the Tibetans, our house was the last to be built.'

She led the way into one of the chalets. 'You needn't worry. Most of the children are away. We try to send them back to their own countries for the summer holidays.'

The basic unit in the village is the 'house-family'. Each chalet has children of only one nationality. The house-parents, one of them a teacher, together with one or two other helpers, are from the same land as the children. Primary school is held in each house in the morning, and children follow their own national curriculum. After primary school they may be prepared for national advanced examinations as well as attending the local 'high school'.

The houses are not only charming, but are designed for their proper function – a secure family life. Going into the hall we found ourselves in what is virtually a 'twin house'. On one side of the hall is the living-room, with tiled stove, wooden floors and walls. A small, well-equipped kitchen leads off it, so that special national meals may be prepared for 'occasions' and sick children catered for. Upstairs are the office and the schoolroom. On the opposite side of the hall are the bedrooms, with three or four beds for the smaller children and twin-bedded rooms for older ones. Gay curtains, bright rugs, pin-ups, picture books, the evidence of hobbies, varied from house to house. The Italian chalet was as different from the British as both were from the Tibetan. But all were obviously lived in by children.

'How many children to each house?'

'Between fifteen and twenty; boys and girls are as equally divided as possible.'

'Do they keep to themselves?'

'How do they manage about language?'

'What about religion?'

The Swiss guide explained that everyone used their own language in their own house, but quickly became familiar with each other's. German, the cantonal language, was the official

village language and that of higher education. Religion, like
everything else, was a part of the life of each house. For the
British children, an Anglican chaplain from Zurich visited the
house. Protestant children attended church in Trogen; Catholics had a little farther to go. By chance, not design, there
were no Jews; and the Tibetan house-father was a Buddhist
lama. We had already seen him with the children as we arrived.

The names of the houses are a delight. *Jukola, Butendiek,
Les Cigales, Pinocchio, Stepping Stones;* they belonged to the
children's world. There is a three-year international secondary-
school course in the new school opened in 1960. In addition
there is a workshop, a kindergarten, a library and an excellent
auditorium or assembly hall.

In the basement of the chalet we had seen rows of boots and
overshoes, and skis piled in the corner. It was easy to imagine
the whole village and the hill slopes a whirling, intercrossing
mass of boys and girls in the winter snows. To live in Pestalozzi
is both adventure and education in international living. They
have 'adventure courses' in Switzerland itself but it is living
together that counts. Every child remains a citizen of his own
country, and will return to it. They leave to become engineers
or pastry-cooks, dressmakers or multi-lingual typists, but they
carry in their baggage the village's 'Certificate of Citizenship'.
More important, they carry in their hearts a belief, founded on
experience, that the things that divide the nations are the false
creations of men's fears, and that national treasures shared can
become the riches of the whole world.

Pestalozzi, as a new village, was given the name of one of
Switzerland's great educational pioneers. It was a name we
were to recall on Lake Lucerne.

Trogen is a small town, known because of the Children's
Village. St Gallen, by contrast, is an old city grown important
because of the industry that surrounds it. Solid, plebeian and

respectable, its shopping streets were gay with flags and its trams crowded with workmen going home. This north-eastern area of Switzerland is the industrial heart of the land, where prosperity does not depend on the tourist trade but on the technology and precision-skills which 'Made in Switzer-land' guarantees all over the world.

Those visitors who do come, come for the abbey. Named after Gallus, an Irish saint who built his cell here in 612, the present great twin-towered church was erected in 1756. Its rococo interior was rather spoiled for us because it was being repainted in the pale blue of a thrush's egg, and the 'marble' pillars, also being repainted, turned out to be only cleverly grained wood. None of this mattered. It was for the abbey's library that we stopped, for this is probably the most priceless collection of mediaeval manuscripts in Europe. And its inlaid wood floor is cherished as much as the books themselves, for we had to put on cloth overshoes very much like those in which unbelievers enter a Muslim mosque. They serve the double purpose of preserving the wood and keeping it polished! 'The finest rococo interior in Switzerland', they say, and the Swiss, who provide leaflets about everything from mediaeval libraries to mountain railways, thoughtfully had a leaflet about the library – for sale, of course, not free – which even repro-duced the intricate pattern of the floor. It informed us that there are to be found here 100,000 books, 2,000 handwritten manuscripts and a unique collection of 1,700 incunabula. The word, with its shivery witchcraft sound, means only early printed books.

In the square by the abbey is a statue to Valdez, the Protestant reformer and humanist. The Swiss see nothing incongruous in a Protestant statue only a stone's throw from a Catholic abbey . . . and equally nothing odd that, not far away, is a statue to commemorate the inauguration of the town's water supply.

My time sequence has slipped through comparing Trogen and St Gallen. It was really the following morning that we explored the abbey. Our only thought on arrival was a hotel, a wash and some tea.

'Oh, no!'

We all said it at the same time. Talk of the *Sonnenspitze* at Ehrwald . . . only the previous night . . . and now this! Surely it must be the dullest, greyest and squarest of all hotels in St Gallen. Ungenerously and instinctively we christened it the Y.M.C.A.

I could not pick out the *hotelier*, amongst the locals sitting at the red and black checked cloths, until a stout, untidy man in braces and no tie got up at the end of his hand of cards. He greeted us in perfect English, gave us the keys of our rooms, hoped we would be comfortable and showed us where the stairs were. A boy was already waiting to carry our bags. Half way up the stairs a door opened into a huge ballroom which looked exactly like a parish hall when the caretaker was on holiday – even to bits of bunting hanging loosely on a nail. On the landing outside a glass-fronted cupboard was filled with trophies, cups, badges and pennants, all covered with dust, and looking like the relics of a regimental mess. They were, in fact, the relics of the 'St Gallen Volunteers'. No doubt they held their revels in the ballroom. We speculated on the rank of our stout host.

We had no complaints about our large, Victorian bedrooms but did not feel like having dinner served off checked table-cloths by a large man in braces. Fussy, that's all we were! We drove away to find somewhere else, turned this way and that – obviously we were not going to escape from industrial St Gallen – and ended up at a pleasant-looking hotel with a swinging sign of a golden sun. We went in.

Inside, the woodwork was dark. The cloths were checked in red and black. A few locals were drinking mild beer. And the host, behind the small bar, was in braces. We laughed – at ourselves and industrial St Gallen – and were immediately at home.

The meal was excellent, with soup in a silver tureen and the *Schnitzel* sizzling hot on a silver salver. The old man with his wrinkled wife at the next table raised his glass to us with a friendly smile, and the waitress was ready to stop and chat. In the middle of our dinner the door was flung open and six firemen, in black uniform, big helmets, hatchets at their sides and the grimy faces of men who had done their duty, tramped in, through the little restaurant and out at the back. Where to and why we never found out.

On the wall was a large gold medal, with a citation from a national exhibition. When we asked our host what it was for he expanded even more – which is saying a good deal.

'Come and see,' he invited us. Across the passage he opened a door into a butcher's shop. The combination of *Gasthof* and *Metzgerei* is to be noted and commended. We were not surprised the meat had been good. But the butcher's pride was already in his hands. Ripe red sausages, made of pork, beef and water. Succulent white ones of veal and milk. He held out the white ones.

'It was for these that I got the gold medal!'

Don't forget to see Sister Olga Frischknedt, Kantonal Hospital.
Ten o'clock seemed a bit late to start hospital visiting, but our friend Arthur Hutchinson had been insistent before we left home, twice underlining *Don't Forget*. There would be no time next day. Twenty minutes later, ready to risk a snub, we pulled up at the hospital. Inside, a figure advanced on us who seemed to be half nurse, half nun. The long, dark blue dress and the neat cap belonged to the nurse, the calm face to the nun. Apparently not even surprised at a social call at such an hour she went away to call Sister Olga.

In some ways it was the strangest hour of our whole holiday.

With the patients mostly asleep, we looked into one dim-lit ward after another as the clock ticked on. Sister Olga was very slight, light of voice and gesture, gentle and gay. She had stayed with our friends in England, but we hardly needed such common grounds to become friends. Like the sister on the stairs, her dress was severe. Her face, on the other hand, had the serenity of the dedicated *religieuse* and the sense of fun that so often goes with it. Half nurse and half nun was an accurate description, but her Order was not a Catholic one. She was a Methodist Deaconess, vowed to the same compassion and self-lessness as those outside her own Church.

We talked in her room for a long time, and she waved away our apologies at keeping her so late. In the end she would not let us go without seeing one thing more.

'You *must* see my babies.'

So, at midnight, we followed her quiet footsteps along the empty corridor. She opened a door and beckoned us in. Tiny sighs rose all round the big room, and here and there a gentle whisper. We began to count the cots, but Sister Olga antici-pated us.

'Sixty,' she said. 'Aren't they lovely?'

Back in the hotel we really noted the wardrobe for the first time. It was super-colossal, a Swiss Victorian monster.

'What's in it?'

We opened the door and found it full of shelves. Shelves and boxes. Intrigued, we peered into the cardboard cartons. Every one was full of Christmas decorations. As I lay in the dark I thought I heard the vigorous strains of the Volunteers' band playing old-fashioned dances at their Christmas party. The sound of *Schweizer-deutsch* voices echoed up the stone staircase. My last thought as I went to sleep was of our host in the decorated ballroom stripping off his regimental jacket to exert himself with greater ease in his braces.

WE WERE hoping for snow peaks and blue water. Instead, Lucerne was in its most perverse weather-mood, with the lovely lake a deep green and Pilatus, which holds the tormented soul of Pontius Pilate, only a shrouded silhouette. By next day even the green lake had darkened to sombre black. But Lucerne weather is a national gibe, a sort of Swiss Manchester, as a guidebook for the Swiss themselves points out. 'There *are* optimistic visitors who have been known to go to Lucerne without an umbrella!' Fortunately, the sunshine is never far behind the rain.

It is only an hour or so from St Gallen to Lucerne, but to hurry along, as we did, meant missing things worth seeing. One of them was Einsiedeln, which claims that its pilgrims are second in number only to Lourdes. They come for the same reason, but their case-histories are less closely checked. The tiny 'black Madonna', bedizened with jewelled crowns, is so shrouded in gold and silver vestments that only her black face remains visible. It is for her sake that tens of thousands come to the splendid baroque church. The ornate side-chapels, the gilded altar, the sumptuous decoration are remarkable enough. But it is the sticks, crutches and leg-irons hanging on the walls or piled at the side that catch the eye. Faith gives one reason, psychology another, but there is no doubt that an untold number of the faithful have found healing within sight of the Black Madonna.

In Schwyz, too, a charming town of old houses, we might have stopped with profit. It is here that the original charter of Swiss liberties, the parchment signed in the Rutli meadow, is preserved in the archives of the nation. But, in fact, we did not even stop long for lunch, for the Swiss are hard on roadside picnickers. In a country where cultivable land is scarce and no one is above thinking about money, farmers make use of every square metre. 'Lay-bys' are a waste of good ground. As it was, we were soon within sight of the *Vierwaldstattersee* – the 'lake of the four wooded cantons' – which Britishers call the 'Lake of Lucerne'.

There are people who dislike Lucerne for the same reason they dislike Newquay or Keswick – because so many other people like them, and go there. This is plain snobbery. It is by far the best of the big lakeside towns. It is not as big as Geneva, less Victorian than Lausanne, with more history than Montreux and really on the lake, unlike Interlaken. Its only true competitor, Lugano, vivid and Italianate, lacks the snows of Tiflis and Lucerne's wooded hills. None the less, it might be better than it is. It stands as a memorial to the stupidity of its materialistic, tourist-minded 19th-century burghers. Long after the middle ages it was a city of old inns and twisting streets; 'the city of stork-nests' and of the Carnival of Fritschi, the legendary merrymaker. Less than a hundred years ago the city fathers, afraid that possible visitors would be offended by mediaeval jerry-building and haphazard town-planning, tore down the city gates, all but nine of the wall-towers, some of the bridges and many of the fine old houses. They went on to line the water-frontage with solid and 'splendid' hotels and were able to claim that 'Mark Twain stayed here' and 'Queen Victoria slept here'. The Swiss veneration for Queen Victoria in Lucerne, the Oberland and Lake Geneva is altogether remarkable!

Fortunately, the burghers' enthusiastic vandalism ran down before they entirely destroyed a town that, had it remained, would have matched the best cities on the Romantic Road. A few of the Musegg towers remain. So do the Mill bridge, the Chapel bridge and enough of the lovely old squares and houses by the river Reuss to leave us incensed by the thought of all that is lost.

It was in one of the old houses by the river that we stayed – a tall, yellow-ochre building surmounting a deep arcade which shaded fruit-barrows, flower-sellers and cafés. From the bedroom we looked across the olive-green Reuss, graced by languid swans, to the opposite, tree-lined bank and the Jesuit church.

The Chapel bridge, just outside our hotel, has one hundred and eleven panels, painted with the arms of every patrician family living in Lucerne when it was constructed in 1333. The dog-legged Mill bridge was built a century later, in 1408.

I always think of Lucerne as the town of the Dance of Death. The pitched roof of the Mill bridge was used, like the Kappelbrucke, for a sort of popular art-gallery. Triangular panels, set between the cross-beams and the roof, provided a thoroughgoing exploitation of the popular mediaeval 'dance of death' – that widespread remembrancer that death comes to all men, and often unexpectedly. In pictures whose brilliance has faded through five centuries, you see the skeleton Death sitting with the gambling nobility, mingling with the crowds at a wedding, standing by the ostler as he helps a traveller from his horse at an inn. There is no horror on any of the faces. They go about their business and their pleasure unaware. Originally, it is said, every trade and profession of Lucerne was depicted in these

panels. It must have shaken the urbanity of the patricians to be
so equated with the peasants by the presence of Death. Or
perhaps they chose only to use the Kappelbrucke which
depicted their arms and their nobility. But it is, above everything else, a symbol of Swiss belief in democracy.

Near the bridges, the Water Tower stands in the river. Not
a watch-tower but a beacon-tower, it had a still more gruesome use. Though the city's archives were kept in a room
above water-level, prisoners were kept in a dungeon and the
torture-chamber was on the 'ground' floor.

We explored the farther side of the Reuss and the Jesuit
church – the first baroque church in Switzerland – and crossed back
by the Chapel bridge into the old town. The squares, however
crowded, are still enchanting. The Kappelplatz and Kornmarkt
explain themselves, and so, for that matter, does the Weinmarkt
– though the old mural depicting Christ at the Last Supper gives
a somewhat exaggerated biblical blessing to the local wine trade.

There are many other things to see, if you have time,
including the 'Lion of Lucerne', a gigantic sculpture in the
rock. Carved from a model by Berthel Thorwaldsen, the
Swedish sculptor, the lion is thirty feet long and by it are
recorded the names of twenty-six officers and seven hundred
soldiers, mercenaries in the service of Louis XVI of France.
They died in the defence of the Tuilleries when the revolu-
tionary mob besieged them on 10th August 1792. Non-Swiss
seldom raise much enthusiasm for the lion. It is a little like
expecting the solid Swiss to rhapsodise over Wellington's
monument in St Paul's. But, when you think of it, it is more
surprising that they themselves are so enthusiastic over Swiss
democrats dying for a French king.

Near the lion is a glacier garden. And a diorama (the Swiss
and Austrians love dioramas) of the retreat of the French army
from Switzerland in 1870. I have never met British visitors
who enthused about those, either.

There is also, of course, a casino, very well conducted, where the maximum stake is one franc.

Window-shopping after dinner I found a sudden sympathy with those who say Lucerne is too crowded. Lancashire, Midland and Scots accents passed by in droves, mixed with Scandinavian and German, heavily laced with American. The shops were too expensive for those on a British tourist allowance and we drifted down through the Kappelplatz to the waterfront, and out of the congestion. The lights on the lake and the reflections in the water were enchanting. The watertower and the Musegg towers were lit with amber light and the twin spires of the Hofkirche were ethereal against a sky growing steadily more menacing.

Inside the Hofkirche, properly the collegiate church of St Leodegar, there was a continuing whisper as the worshippers, dotted about the great church, told their beads, preparing for the next morning's mass. All was dim except for an almost eerie light on the great cross above the altar. As we left the church a forked tongue of brilliant light zigzagged across the sky, from far above Pilatus down to the surface of the lake. On the heels of the lightning came the thunder, beginning to rattle again before the echoes had died away. The sky was cut about by patterns of dazzling light and the thunder turned into an uncreasing reverberation amongst the mountains. It came from every direction, and it was impossible to separate origin and echo. We were engulfed by the noise and half-blinded by the lightning which fantastically illuminated lake, town and mountains. Almost at once the deluge began. It was an hour before we could escape from the café into which we fled for shelter. Mountain storms in Switzerland are unforgettable, especially at night.

By itself, the town of Lucerne is probably worth no more than a half-day coach outing from another centre. It is for the

lake that visitors come and stay – the long vista of the prome-
nade; the jagged mass of Pilatus; the succession of small resorts
grown out of smaller villages on its shores; the woodlands that
sweep thickly down the mountainside. But if it is impossible
to think of Lucerne without thinking of the lake, it is equally
impossible to think of the lake without recalling the history of
this self-sufficient, martial nation.

It was here that the nation really began.

The prehistoric lake-dwellers and the Romans have their
share in the Swiss story but until the 13th century 'Switzerland'
was non-existent; only an agglomeration of separate cantons
subject to the over-lordship of Austria. It was in August 1291,
that the magistrates of the three lakeside cantons of Uri,
Schwyz and Unterwalden met in the meadow at Rutli, at the
farther end of the Lake of Lucerne. There they made a secret
pact of unity which has established Rutli as a far more sacred
spot than Runnymede is to the British. A document was
drawn up in Latin with three seals and the signatures of the
cantonal representatives. It is this parchment which is preserved
at Schwyz, and which marks the beginning of Switzerland as
we know it today.

In 1332 Lucerne joined the League of the Vierwaldstattersee.
At that time the city had only a thousand inhabitants, a small
company indeed to join in the challenge to the might of the
Hapsburg rulers. By 1353, however, the 'confederacy' had
become the 'League of the Eight States' – the new members
being Bern, Glarus, Zurich and Zug. It was becoming evident
to the Austrians that the confederacy must be crushed and, in
1386, Duke Leopold III marched on Lucerne. The forces of the
Eight States met the Duke's army at Lake Sempach on 9th
July. The Duke's forces were not only defeated, but routed.
From that date, Lucerne became a free town and Switzerland
began its march into the free world.

Sempach gave one hero to the nation, Arnold von Winkel-

Pestalozzi Children's Village

. . . for children like these

The Abbey, St Gallen

ried, whose statue is in the market-place at Stans; but it is the
legendary figure of William Tell who has passed into European
folklore.

Three places on the lake are linked with the Tell story.
Altdorf, at the end of the lake, where his statue stands, is the
scene of 'the boy and the arrow'. It was here that Tell, held as
a suspect rebel, was ordered to shoot the apple off his son's
head. When Gessler, the Hapsburg's local *Gauleiter*, saw a
second arrow remaining in Tell's quiver after the crossbow
was lowered, he asked what it was for.

'*You*,' answered Tell, 'had I hurt my son!'

Thrown into a boat to be taken down the lake and imprisoned, he lay bound until a storm blew up across the lake
and only then, to save their lives, did his captors release him to
steer them to safety. He made a landfall at Tellsplatte – 'Tell's
Meadow' – where he leapt ashore and escaped.

The third of the 'Tell sites' is nearer to Lucerne, on the
opposite side of the lake to Tellsplatte, at Kussnacht. Here he
waited after his escape and, in a narrow lane, shot Gessler with
the arrow he had reserved for him.

It all happened in 1307. Or did it? Few Swiss would now
accept the stories as history. Tell, however, personifies the
spirit of the men of the Rutli meadow – and of that event there
is no historic doubt. Yet, strangely, the sacred meadow remained private property until 1859, and it was not until a
prospective purchaser revealed that he intended to build a
hotel on it that an appeal was launched to the nation. The
price was 55,000 Swiss francs, and the appeal raised 95,199
francs. From that time Rutli meadow has been a place of pilgrimage, and thousands of schoolchildren are taken every year
to venerate the spot where their liberty began.

Much more recently the meadow was chosen as a place
where those liberties were reaffirmed. On 25th July 1940,
when Belgium and France had fallen, and the little nation was

K

surrounded by German, Austrian and Italian forces, the
Commanding General of the Swiss Armies summoned every
unit commander to meet him at the sacred meadow. Here the
defence plans were expounded to the leaders of an army that
remained on the alert until the Germans finally signed their
capitulation in the Technical College at Rheims.

We did not get as far as Rutli the next morning, but we did
want a trip on the lake. Armed with picnic basket and rain-
coats we presented ourselves at the booking office on the quay.
I asked for four tickets to Weggis.

The man in the kiosk, seeming by every brass button a
sailor, looked us over carefully.

'Are these your own children?'

The 'children' looked outraged. I myself was more outraged
by the next question.

'The lady *is* your wife, sir? Not a housekeeper? A friend,
perhaps?'

I silently offered him our passports but he put them aside. 'It
is not a question of morals, sir. Only of money.'

When I asked if I could not go on the lake with somebody
else's wife he looked quizzical and pulled his stumpy beard.
'Of course. But then you can't have a family ticket!' Even
better than a Swiss Holiday Ticket, if you can get it. Four
for the price of two and a half. Self, wife and two children – of
any age under twenty-one. But the lady *must* be your wife,
and you must not have adopted the children for the occasion.
The man stared at me. 'You thought I was being rude? Surely
not. We only want to help our visitors. With the Family
Ticket you may make five journeys. On anything. Steamers,
funiculars, cable-cars—'

'Even the Jungfrau railway?'

'Certainly! Now, you are going to Weggis. . . .' He took
agreement for granted, wrote our names in the little books,

took one form out of each book, issued our tickets and wished us a good trip.

It was only on the boat that I discovered he had issued us with first-class tickets when I had intended to get seconds.

They are small, compact steamers that ply the twenty-four miles from Lucerne to Fluelen, crossing and recrossing the lake to make the mileage almost double. It was on 1st December 1835 that a Lucerne merchant named Knorr informed the inhabitants that he intended to establish a shipping company. Three years later the *City of Lucerne* made her first trip. The canton of Uri forbade it to land because it would deprive boatmen of their trade, and at Fluelen it was stoned for the same reason. The opposition did not last long and, today, the steamer trip is a day's delight.

The loudspeaker gives you all the information you need.

'On the left is Seeburg, with the Polytechnic chalets.'

'The white villa, there at Tribschen, belonged to Richard Wagner, the great composer.' I thought of mad King Ludwig, Wagner's patron. The loudspeaker does not tell us that Wagner was inspired by birdsong near Zurich for the music of the forest scene in *Siegfried*. Or that the blacksmith at Tribschen first nearly drove the composer mad with his hammer and anvil and then suddenly provided the motif for the *Siegfried* 'forging song'.

The boat swings to port again. 'Queen Victoria stayed here.'

The left arm of the lake goes down towards Kussnacht. 'It was where Queen Astrid was killed in a motor accident.' He does not tell us that the King of the Belgians, who loved the lake as well as his queen, had his villa pulled down stone by stone, and never returned.

Ahead of us rises the Rigi. The commentator does not say that Queen Victoria climbed it. But she did.

Beyond Weggis the steamer ploughed its way into the morning mist towards Gersau. This pleasant village is another

Gotham, like the cheese village of Vorarlberg. All countries
have them – and it is the Gersau people who tell the tale most
often. In the church was a silver bell and, when Napoleon's
army invaded Switzerland, the villagers were anxious not to
lose it. They rowed out into the middle of the lake, dropped
the bell over the side at the deepest point – and marked a cross
on the bottom of the boat so that they could locate it again.

There are many people who prefer these smaller lakeside
resorts to the city itself, though almost anywhere will provide
an excellent touring centre. Engelberg with its monastery,
nestling in the valley below the Tiflis . . . the St Gothard Pass,
Ticino and the langour of the Italian lakes . . . the Three
Passes – Brunig, Grimsel and Furka . . . the whole of the
Oberland . . . all are within easy reach.

One place I *must* mention. Stans, at the foot of the Stanser-
horn, on the arm of the lake opposite to Kussnacht. On the
tower of the church are painted the crossed keys of St Peter –
an acknowledgement that these lakeside cantons provide the
Swiss Guard at the Vatican. In the market-place is Arnold von
Winkelried's statue, surrounded by lances that are renewed as
they perish. It was this knight of Stans who made possible the
Swiss victory at Sempach. The Austrian pikemen were so
solidly massed that it seemed impossible to break their ranks.
It was then that Arnold ran forward, gathered half a dozen
lances in his arms and, as they impaled him to the ground,
made an unexpected gap in the ranks through which the Swiss
cavalry was able to charge, on their way to decisive victory.

But, to me, the finest thing about Stans is the death mask in
its town hall. In this little town, which held out stubbornly
against Napoleon, the French soldiers massacred every man in
the garrison, leaving only the aged and the children. It was at
that time that Heinrich Pestalozzi came to Stans in reply to
their appeal for help. Every educationalist knows his name. He
gathered the children together, founded an orphanage and put

into practice many of his educational theories. Switzerland counts him amongst its greatest sons, and Stans exhibits his death-mask as a tribute to selfless service and compassion.

That is why Dr Corti had no difficulty in finding a name for his new international village. What could it be but 'Pestalozzi'?

Mountains made Easy

THE SWISS approach to tourism has been to make *everything* easy, including mountains – but not to make it cheap. The scenery is free. It is taking a close look at it that costs the money. On the other hand efficiency, politeness and safety are beyond doubt or reproach.

We had planned to spend five days in the Oberland but, as we climbed over the Brunig pass from Lucerne the clouds were low, and so were our spirits. Not even the super-efficiency of the Swiss can guarantee sunshine amongst the mountains. Then, as we came to the little wood-carvers' village of Brienz, the thunderstorm passed over. Just behind the village rises the Brienzer Rothorn. I shall never forget my first sight of the panoramic view from the top – but it is no trip for a cloud-wrapped day. Across the Brienz Lake are the Rauchenbach Falls where Conan Doyle had his – to him, boring – hero, Sherlock Holmes, flung to death by Moriarty. Conan Doyle was as surprised by the readers' clamour to resurrect him as were the Swiss themselves by the fancy-dress tour of the Holmesites to the Falls in 1968!

Interlaken, lying on the flat land between Lake Brienz and Lake Thun, must be one of the dullest towns in Switzerland – if not the dullest. Created in Victorian and Edwardian days to house the tourists, it has nothing of history, culture or architecture to commend it – not even a good museum or an art gallery. It is not for any of these things that people come here, after all! We swept through it and up towards the edge of the mountains, to the *Gasthof* in Wilderswil whose colourful postcard was on the front seat.

The reality was a shock. It had none of its colour-transparency look as it sat on the edge of the road, at the end of the village, with only a view of misty fields. The atmosphere, inside and out, was cold and clammy and when I came back upstairs from registering I found the other three undecided whether to leave, or weep and unpack. My suggestion that we were tired with travelling produced a storm like that on the Brunig.

But we stayed.

We had a better dinner than we had hoped for, unpacked reluctantly and played canasta till bedtime. Like a good courier, I read up a bit on Switzerland. Area: 16,000 square miles. Population: 5½ million; ¼ million engaged in farming; ¾ million engaged in tourism. National revenue . . .

What was the good of cold facts? We wanted to see the mountains.

I put the book down and went to sleep.

When I wakened the sun was brilliant and the sky was blue. Up the Lauterbrunnen valley the fields were rice-green and and the woods almost black in the early sunlight. At the head of the valley, hanging ethereal like a gossamer theatre-drop, was the gleaming whiteness of the Jungfrau. I called to my wife; went in and hauled Susan and Paul out of bed and on to the verandah, watching their faces.

Outside, the little *Gasthof* reproduced its postcard colours –

the old brown of the chalet, the red of the geraniums on our verandah and in the boxes by the doors. Inside, Herr – let me call him Schmidt – was smoking a black cigar and humming a mountain rhythm through his teeth. On the table was a basket piled with home-made rolls; a silver jug of coffee; honey as well as cherry jam. Erna, the diminutive waitress, was infected by the air and smiled gaily at us.

Afterwards, we walked across the fields into Interlaken. Though it still looked infinitely dull it was obvious why visitors have flocked here for a century. The mountains stand high round it and, across the parkland in the centre of the town, rising between the dark cleft of the Lauterbrunnen valley, the Jungfrau, remote and incredibly beautiful, dominates everything else. It is, without question, one of the unforgettable sights of Europe. Even so, we still preferred Wilderswil to Interlaken. The Unspunnen castle huddles against the trees. The Lutschine river, white with snow-water, rattles past it. The houses and hotels are truly Swiss – chalets old and new, but not Victoriana. We sat on our verandah to write postcards.

'Queer they don't put "Switzerland" on their stamps, or whatever it is in French or German or something!'

But that – I had the figures from last night's guide-book browsing – was the trouble. German, or French, or what? 70 per cent speak German (or Schweizer-deutsch); 20 per cent French; 9 per cent Italian; and 1 per cent the ancient Latin tongue, Romanisch. The democratic spirit is not to be disregarded. Where everyone cannot share, choose none of them. The major tribe of Roman Switzerland was the *Helvetiae*. So, on the stamps, *Helvetia* it is – and no one is outraged. For the same reason the international letter-plate is 'CH': *Confederatione Helvetiae*.

After lunch we drove up the valley to Lauterbrunnen, alongside the twin rivers – the White Lutschine, fed by snow, and the Black, by glaciers. A thin waterfall, the Staubach, drops a single thread of water from the precipice behind the village. Farther up the valley the Trummelbach Falls thunder down *inside* the mountain with incredible ferocity, awesome and deafening. Apart from this, Lauterbrunnen is no more than a parking-place, and a junction for the trains which come from Interlaken and transfer their passengers to the first major stage of the Jungfrau railway. But that is a whole day's outing, and we chose the ruler-straight funicular to Murren.

The 'folk tale' of all funiculars is of the lady who asked what would happen if the brakes failed. The 'corny' answer was that there was a second brake – and if that failed all would depend on the kind of life you had lived. They never fail. Cable cars rise and fall smoothly throughout summer and winter. Railways run with impeccable regularity through terrain which taxes every ingenuity of the engineers' skill. Only someone as knowledgeable as my friend Cecil J. Allen, doyen of railway writers, in such a book as *Switzerland's Wonderful Railways*, can pay proper tribute to them. They are so improbably perfect that the rest of the world takes them for granted.

Murren clusters on a shelf half-way up the mountain, and is sited on the top of a precipice. Miniature on the opposite side of the valley, Wengenalp clings to a similar shelf, slightly sloping as if it might well tilt the chalets into Lauterbrunnen below. Far above us the great mountains, the Monch, the Eiger and their terrible companions, rose ravishingly white against the deep blue sky. With ravines and dipping snowfields etched in pale blue light, they held us spellbound, and brought us to a stop again and again as we walked through the village. For such a sight as this it would have been worth enduring day upon day of yesterday's cloud and mist.

This is not really a summer resort and the massive hotels were shuttered and hollow, waiting for the end of summer and the coming of the snow. It is then that this village, early popularised by the British, is truly itself. One summer event, however, has caught the eye of the world through television – the Balloon Race. The village doctor, an elderly man in plus-fours and yellow stockings, with a mountain-darkened face, took us home and showed us the plateau in front of his house where the giant circles are laid out, slowly inflated, and then take off over the great Alps towards Italy.

Usually the mountain air left us too tired to do very much in the evenings but this night we spent at the Interlaken *Kursaal*. We felt Queen Victoria would have enjoyed it – she once stayed at Interlaken, too. Coated with gilt, gleaming with crystal, hung with chandeliers, the huge *salon* was like the 'folk evening' itself – decorous, self-conscious and dull. The performance was in two halves, and the second almost exactly reproduced the first. The entrance ticket stated *Drinks are Obligatory* – but two cups of coffee or one bottle of wine sufficed for most of the audience. The interval was introduced by a suave announcement that 'You may enjoy yourselves in the gaming-room', but it did not seem to me that the casino made much money from the few people round the table staking their statutory maximum single franc. The Swiss, in any case, only bet on certainties.

The most interesting item on the programme – again, done twice – was the flag-throwing – a skill which looks almost too easy as the 'thrower' flings the flag up, down and about without its ever becoming tangled or furled. The national flag, white cross on red ground, the flag of Schwyz where the dream of Swiss liberty first began, must be exactly four feet square and made of pure silk. Probably few who watch the demonstration realise that they are seeing the historical relic of the 'drum-major', whose task it was to walk ahead of the regiment, flinging the flag high enough to be seen by the whole 'line of march'.

The contrast between man-made entertainment and natural beauty is stark and sober in the Oberland. We had had enough 'production folk-lore' to last us for some time. Expensive though it was, we decided we must see the Jungfrau – and, at five pounds a ticket (reduced by the Swiss Holiday one) it *is* expensive.

'It just *can't* be worth it!' We have a proper sense of money-values in our family, and the comment seemed fair enough.

Next morning the Jungfrau had disappeared behind the clouds, and we went to Grindelwald instead.

I hope I have not put anyone 'off' Interlaken! You may not want to stay long inside it, but there is no centre in the country which offers more *outside*. The local hills, the Schynigge Platte and the Heimwehfluh, are a morning's jaunt. Mountain villages – Grindelwald, or Kandersteg with the Oeschenen Valley and the Blue Lake, for instance – take only an afternoon. Bern in one direction and Lucerne in the other are only half-day or full-day trips. Montreux, with the Chillon castle, is at the end of the Blue Arrow train route, while the Red Arrow takes you over the St Gotthard pass to Lugano. You can fill every day of a week, or a fortnight, and still not have had time to go on a steamer trip on both lakes, Brienz and Thun.

Of all the 'possibles' we decided on Grindelwald, a typical mountain village, unspoiled by modern building, where even the highest Hilton would be cut down to size by the mountains. Only the Grindelwald glacier and the harsh, relentless face of the Eiger showed now and again in the drifting mist. Even so, the air was crisp, clean and almost inebriating as we swung up the longest chair-lift in the world to First (which is pronounced Feerst) at four for the price of two-and-a-half again. Below us isolated chalets were dotted amongst the fields. Men and women worked unconcernedly as we hoisted over them, or puttered about on miniature tractors pulled behind tiny two-wheeled engines. One thing particularly intrigued my wife, and in a quiet café she could no longer contain her curiosity.

'How *do* they manage in those chalets? They're so remote. And there aren't any shops up there, surely?'

The proprietor pointed down to the lower valley at the foot of the glacier. 'Down there it's not so bad. They have two shops. But you're right. It's more difficult up on the hills. Not only no shops – there aren't any roads, either, or even paths. But you may have seen those little two-wheeled engines.'

'With a tractor behind?'

'Sometimes. The engine is detachable. It can draw a manure-sprayer or a corn-cutter. Or a cart. By law a farmer is allowed to drive across the fields for food, fuel, stores and so on.'

'Oh. And if he just wants to take his family out for the afternoon? Or go to the inn?'

The restaurateur was crisp. 'Then he walks.' He smiled at our wry faces. 'Things are better than they used to be, though, before there were any engines.' He beckoned us to the window. 'They're a lot better on the mountains, too. Look! You can just see the Wetterhorn in the mist. If it were clear you could see the mountain huts that the climbers use at night. Until recently they had to have carriers for the provisions to keep the huts well stocked.'

'They don't drive the engines up the mountain!'

He laughed with us. 'Not quite, no. They use helicopters to drop provisions instead. We live in a new world today, *mein Herr.*'

'Where do the helicopters come from?'

'Thun. From the "Mountain Aviation Service". They're mostly used for rescues when there have been bad falls – but the pilots can do almost anything in the mountains.'

Outside, the street seemed to have suddenly filled with the chorus from the Kursaal's 'folk night'. Men and women were climbing out of a coach, rather solemn but obviously enjoying themselves. The men in flat black hats and red-and-black coats cut like mess-jackets; the women in high lace haloes or small stiff coronets while, at the back, their embroidered blouses had thin silver chains hanging from neck to waist. I recognised it as the cantonal costume of Bern.

'Just up for a day's outing,' commented the café proprietor.

On Sunday, on the lakes or the funiculars, the girls are generally to be found in their cantonal finery. They still wear it without being self-conscious and, in fact, use it very often. The costumes vary widely between the cantons, and a visitor can not only get a lot of interest from trying to recognise them; he can also give some real pleasure by saying: 'I see you're from Valais' or wherever it is. As long as he gets it right! It may not be worth the risk unless he is sure.

Only the glacier's foot showed below the mist as we set off for Wilderswil. Mark Twain, in his *Innocents Abroad*, wrote about sitting on a glacier because he had been told it was moving, and getting off again when he found it only moved an inch a year. But there was a time when the inhabitants of Grindelwald believed it was advancing so fast that it would engulf the village.

That was in 1719, and they paid 'a Protestant gentleman from Vaud' a considerable sum to exorcise it. The danger passed for two generations. Then, in 1777, the terror seized them again. This time they tried a famous exorcist from Sarnen, but the holy monk was more cautious than the Protestant gentleman. He asked the village council to decide whether the advance was the work of God or the devil. Since the council was equally divided, and a different set of spells was needed in each case, the monk refused to take the risk and left the villagers to their fate.

Glacier and village are still there – but the Grindelwald glacier, like most other glaciers in Switzerland, grows smaller year by year.

Back in our *Gasthof* Herr Schmidt was interested to know we had been to Grindelwald. 'I was a cook there for twenty years.' He named one of the big hotels. That accounted for the quality of our meals, and I asked him if he had been all afternoon in the kitchen. His English was poor and my German no better, so we had to keep to French.

'I have been shooting. Some cantonal sports.' He gestured to two large cupboards in the bar. One had a collection of medals; the other was crowded with vases, plaques, ribbons and silver bowls. 'I am fond of shooting,' he admitted. It was one of the most remarkable understatements I had heard!

There was one other question we *had* to ask.

'Will it be fine enough for the Jungfrau tomorrow?'

'*Mais oui. Certainement!*'

It was. Brilliantly and unbelievably fine. We were on the train at Lauterbrunnen by seven-thirty.

The 'Jungfrau excursion' is too well known to justify a long description. To do so, in any case, would need a whole chapter – and would pay as much attention to the marvellous engineering of the railways as to the scenery itself. It is almost enough to say that, of all the possible excursions anywhere in Switzerland, this is beyond question the most outstanding and memorable, and worth every centime of the fare. There is no part of the day – and it is no half-day trip – which has not its own wonder. The splendour of the peaks as we climbed from Wengenalp to the Kleine Scheidegg, where we changed to the Jungfrau railway . . . the forbidding Eiger glacier . . . the view of the Eismeer, the Sea of Ice . . . then the Jungfraujoch itself, the 'saddle of the Jungfrau', with its ice-palace and the cold blue corridors leading out into the snow. A small aircraft was taking off at intervals from the snowy plateau in the saddle. Tyros were buckling on skis for a tentative skid downwards, and huskies plodded up and down the slope with their sledges. The sun beat down on the snow so that even a towelling shirt was hot.

Above everything else – the mountains. Eiger, Monch, Jungfrau, Schrechhorn, Wetterhorn, Breithorn, Lauteraarhorn, Fischerhorn, Tschingelhorn, Finsteraarhorn, Ebnehfluh ... every name is magical, every one over 12,000 feet and most over 13,000 – apart from the Himalayas, the most formidable range of snow-covered peaks in the world.

In the restaurant an American lady, unbelievably, sat writing postcards, resisting every persuasion of her daughter to come and see.

'I've simply *got* to get these into the post right now so that they're postmarked up here!'

She added another to the stack before her.

Her train went twenty minutes later. She nearly missed it and she never saw the snows – but she caught the post.

It is no wonder Switzerland is full of visitors.

It has been so for centuries.

It has opened its frontiers to refugees of all kinds, not only to the children at Pestalozzi.

Wagner sheltered here from Prussia; Garibaldi, Mazzini and Mussolini from Italy; Bakunin, Trotsky and Lenin from Russia.

Writers as varied as John Evelyn, Byron, Shelley, Hans Andersen and Somerset Maugham have made their homes here or passed slowly through it. So have composers as widely different as Brahms, Beethoven and Stravinsky. Beethoven used the theme of the Rigi alpenhorn-blower in his *Pastoral Symphony*, and Wagner took his cue for one of Isolde's arias from the same horn. Brahms gave the horns in his *C Minor Symphony* the very theme which the alpenhorn plays today on the path between Grindelwald and the Kleine Scheidegg. Stravinsky turned from nature to men and machines, and found one of the principal subjects in *Les Noces* when he was travelling on a funicular and heard two drunken men saying the same phrase over and over again, more and more loudly against the clatter of the cog-wheels.

Perhaps it is as well for Swiss pride that not everybody praises it. It is true that Charlie Chaplin had his villa outside Lausanne, but a more literary humourist, Bret Harte, described it as a country which perpetually gave him a headache or a stomache-ache. Dostoevsky was more curt. 'Everything . . . is really dreadful!'

Bret Harte might have been up the Jungfrau, judging by his symptoms, though I can hardly believe it of Dostoevsky.

For ourselves, everything – except, perhaps, the hotels where Queen Victoria stayed and the cut-glass museum that passes for the Interlaken Kursaal – everything was wonderful.

15) *Ça Va!*

THE NIESEN was powdered with fresh snow as we drove up the lakeside towards Thun on the Friday morning. The little towns on the northern shore were clean and inviting across the blue water . . . Merligen, with its pilgrim-way to the grotto of St Beatus, the missionary to the whole region . . . Sigiswil, with dairy-farms and cattle-breeding . . . Gunten, with its waterfall . . . Hinterfingen, oddly famous both as a centre for yachting and pansy-nurseries. The high mountains drew steadily away behind us.

Wherever you first see the Oberland peaks they linger in your memory. I first saw them from Thun, with the unforgettable trio of Monk, Maiden and Ogre rose-pink in the evening sky – and I have had an affection for Thun ever since. The lower town by the lake is charming, and dominated by a solid castle. You may like to know that it has the oldest medallion carpet in Switzerland and also a Gothic antependium! This is apparently a veil for the front of an altar, but I never knew they had Gothic ones! I found it more intriguing that Fennimore Cooper, author of *The Last of the Mohicans,*

L

once marched past the castle in the ranks of the Swiss army. Probably he marched past others, too, but the locally printed guidebook makes it appear a unique distinction.

We had cancelled our booking at Bern, deciding to press farther on and ease our journey home – which was a pity, for it is a town to linger in. The Parliament House, described as 'a fine building' – which means it is neither better nor worse than most of its kind – and set above the river Aare, offers a quite spectacular panorama of the Oberland. The restaurants are numerous and excellent, as you would expect in a capital city with over sixty embassies and legations. Its shops are elegant, restrained – and expensive. But it was to the old city that we turned for an hour or so before pushing on, for it is full of lovely things round which the life of the capital moves purposefully and profitably. Of its eleven fountains, ten date from the 16th century. Its bridges are almost as old, and so are many of its houses and towers. No one should miss the splendidly decorative clock-tower and most people will want to look into the bear-pit. The first bears were brought here by a prince of the city, centuries ago, and they have clowned here ever since. The name of the town, and its cantonal emblem, derives from them. Once more, as I always do, I wished we could have stayed longer.

Beyond Bern we might have been in another land. The most notable changes were the loss of the great mountains and the lavish fertility of the countryside. Amongst the woodlands and the little hills the farmlands were superlatively rich. No grass had been greener, no corn more golden in all our travels. We felt the vegetables would be of 'county show' size and the fruit luxuriant. The farmhouses, too, were astonishingly large – immense chalets, with a sort of frontal apse overhung by the roof, barns built on to the back and cart-houses added to the side. The productivity of the land was explained when we stopped to have a closer look.

A tractor, with a 'tanker' behind it, was stationed outside a farm and I got out to inspect it all. Inside the building was a gargantuan tank, from which rich, deep liquid was being pumped into the tanker. I suppose one can get used to anything – but a well-filled pond of odorous liquid manure must necessitate strong stomachs, even if it is at the opposite end of the house. I was back in the car quicker than I had left it!

From the exuberant countryside the sprayed fertilizers, made yet richer by the hot sunshine, penetrated the car, until we climbed out of the farming country and looked down on the limpid greenness of Lake Neuchâtel.

The town stretches for two and a half miles along the lake. It has some relics of prehistoric lake dwellings; few remains of the Romans who founded it; a 12th-century castle; an exquisite renaissance 'Maison des Halles'; an 18th-century château, the Palais du Peyrou. But, despite two thousand years of history, Neuchâtel is a town of today. They claim better French is spoken here than in France, which is why it has so many 'finishing-schools'. Its university is internationally notable and its intellectual atmosphere contemporary, while its considerable industry does nothing to spoil or dirty the town. The vineyards on the terraced hills are the reason for its going *en fête* when the grapes are ripe. It is, indeed, only at the *fêtes* that the Swiss towns – even bourgeois Bern – prove by their gaiety and abandon that their solemn faces are only a mask, after all.

Like Zürich, Neuchâtel is a watch-making centre, and the Swiss Watchmaking Laboratory is situated here. The title sounds staid in English, and taut in French. Only in German is full sonorous justice done to it: *Schweitzerische Laboratorium für Uhrmacherieforschungen!*

'Forty kilometres, and we're out of Switzerland.' Paul was acting as navigator again. Both he and Susan were excellent.

'Last country – and last lap!'

Above Lake Neuchâtel we began to climb. The French call

this region *Franche-Comte*, 'the Free Country'. Most people call
it the Jura, though they do not remember that the words come
from *juria*, the Latin word for 'forests'. It is indeed a land of
mountain and forest, and more 'free for all' than most of
Switzerland or France. Freely, the rivers twist through its
ravines – the Doubs, the Ognan and the Aine; fish swim briskly
in the cold waters; hare, roebuck and wild deer roam plenti-
fully but elusively. Anglers, hunters, climbers – especially
parties of schoolboys – and skiers all make free of the untamed
countryside.

Within a dozen kilometres we passed through the 'arc de
triomphe', more grey and weatherworn than many Roman
ones, in Pontarlier.

Pontarlier could be nowhere else but France. The shops – a
world away from the luxurious displays of Bern – were utterly
mediocre. The buildings were shabby and the shoppers drab.
The little corner café where we asked for tea had two empty
tables outside. Inside, three men played with a greasy pack of
cards and another four were busy with dominoes. They wore
berets and a hunched air of concentration.

This casual, untidy, unpainted face of the French towns and
villages was to be with us almost until we reached the coast.
There were exceptions, but they were few. Their atmosphere,
slightly suspicious, withdrawn and threadbare, was a chilling
contrast with the affluence of Switzerland and Germany.

It is always well to yield to temptation when you see the
sign *route touristique*. Forgetting our unhappy Belgian border
experience we did so beyond Pontarlier where two roads, both
for Ornans, forked ahead of us. Even so, we were not prepared
for the majestic drive of the next few miles along the edge of the
Jura. The route was along a road clinging desperately to the
mountain-face high above the tiny river Loue amongst the
trees. Then, with a twist in the road, the valley opened out

below and ahead. Heavily forested, the gorge became deeper and deeper as it cut away into the mountains, a green canyon which left us speechless. We pulled into a wide lay-by, placed at the most breath-taking viewpoint of the magnificent road, and looked far down the precipice on the Source of the Loue. It was a long time before we set off again for Besançon.

For once we had no booking, but the ease with which the Tourist Office found one for us proved that those people may be right who say you do not need one. Our small private hotel was just across the river, and the proprietor – who sat in the hotel lobby while his wife controlled the restaurant round the corner – greeted us vociferously in a dialect too local to follow closely. He went away, opened another door to let us in, and showed us into what appeared to be a flat belonging to somebody else. It was all very curious but very comfortable, and the simple meal in his wife's restaurant down the side-road was something to remember. Vegetable soup, fish from the Jura rivers, ices, cheese made in this famous cheese town, and *vin ordinaire* decanted above the counter sink from a huge earthenware pitcher. What was typically shabby on the outside proved friendly, hospitable and very good indeed inside. It was a lesson we needed to learn.

Besançon, like Luxembourg, Bern and tiny Esch-sur-Sure, was built defensively within the loop of the river. The Doubs sweeps round it, making a pear-shaped island with a stupendous 400-foot precipice at one end of the old town. From the Pont de la Republique, just outside our hotel, we looked across the white water of the weir to this great cliff on which the Romans and those who followed them had built their citadel. It looked impregnable.

Since no one wanted to go sightseeing next morning I left them behind and went on my own. At the top of the street that leads from the Pont de la Republique to the Place de la Revolution – how deeply the Revolution bit into French history – is

the Hôtel de Ville, with an ornate sculptured frontage three
centuries old. But the Grand' rue, running straight from here
to the cathedral and beyond it to the Citadel, is far older. To
walk along it is to dawdle where the Legions marched, for this
is a true Roman road, unbending as the conquerors themselves.
Near the cathedral Rome has left a more visual mark, for
columns, broken arches and sculptures have been gathered into
an open, grassy square. But one thing remains where it was, a
reminder of how much of Rome is to be found in southern
France. A triumphal arch, erected in honour of the Emperor
Marcus Aurelius, frames the pathway leading to the cathedral.

On and near the Grand' rue are the main sights of this pleas-
ing town. Victor Hugo's birthplace stands here still, and so
does that of the brothers Lumière, Auguste and Louis, born in
the 1860's. Every cinema in the world derives from this little
shop where their father had a photographic business, for it was
the brothers Lumière who saw the possibilities of Edison's first
'moving pictures' and produced the earliest *cinematographe*.

Much older than this little shop is a splendid palace in
Spanish style, the Palais Granville, and from the Roman road
I stepped into as delightful a cloistered courtyard and garden
as it is possible to find outside Spain. To enter it from the busy
street is to move at once into the 16th century.

Two other memories I carried away from Besançon.

One was the lovely Fra Bartolomeo painting in the cathedral
of the *Virgin with the Saints*.

The other was formal French comedy.

Two businessmen came along the Grand' rue from opposite
directions, each carrying a briefcase in his right hand. Just by
me, they halted, face to face.

'*Bonjour, m'sieur*,' said the first, putting his briefcase under
his left hand and stretching out his right hand.

'*Bonjour, m'sieur*,' said the second, doing the same. They
shook hands warmly.

'*Ça va?*' asked the first man.

'*Oui,*' said the second. '*Ça va?*'

'*Oui!*' responded the first, taking his briefcase from his arm.

'*Bonjour, m'sieur,*' said the second man, his briefcase in his hand once more.

'*Bonjour, m'sieur,*' replied the first, walking smartly away.

The road from Besançon to the Channel coast could hardly be rated exciting after much of our earlier route. The towns are small, and the villages featureless, compared with half-timbered Germany and the chalets of Austria and Switzerland. But that does not mean they were without interest, or that we wished we had gone back the way we came. Marnay gave us a glimpse of a castle. Gray boasted a renaissance Hôtel de Ville, and little Champlitte another town hall of the same period and a delightful little church. At Langres we made a longer stop to buy provisions and found that Rome had left her mark here, too, ruling the land when France was known as Gaul. We walked on the ramparts where there were towers that the Romans built. But more astonishing was the vista of this out-spread countryside through which the Romans, and many another army, had marched. The level plains, seeming so monotonous, along which we had been speeding, took on another meaning. Spread below us, the flat countryside stretched to the ragged line of the distant horizon. Not even with the field-glasses could we pick out any signs of industry.

This was Champagne.

Most people associate the name with a sparkling wine. Fewer recall it as a wide province of France. It is a name with a curious etymological history. The Romans, in their Latin tongue – it is a mystery that rough, illiterate legionaries dealt so simply with the declensions and conjugations that perplex our own fifth-formers – had a word *campus*. It originally meant 'field'. But in Italian and French its meaning broadened, so that the *campagna* of Italy and the *champagne* of France both came to mean a 'plain'. The Romans, however, had a more specific meaning for *campus* – the *campus Martius*, the training-ground of the legions. This military association developed in strange ways. In English, the 'camp' is the barracks rather than the training-square. Both in French and Italian, however, *campagna* and *champagne* came literally to mean the 'battle-ground'. In England, so far as I know, 'camp' has never had this meaning. But we have anglicised *campagne*, or *champagne*, into 'campaign' to indicate the military operation itself rather than the ground on which it was fought out.

The flat land we overlooked from the battlements of Langres, the province of Champagne, has always meant both 'plain' and 'battlefield'. Its two meanings coalesce here. Not only it is criss-crossed by Roman roads, but defenders and invaders have campaigned for centuries over it. Soissons is one of the historic battlefields of France, but much nearer our own time Rheims and Verdun, together with a long list of shattered towns and villages, have witnessed campaigns that are part of 20th-century history and tragedy.

Across this undulating plain, whose chalk base makes the grapes of Champagne what they are, we drove on relentlessly. One score of kilometres piled on to the last. The earth was reddish; the corn yellow; the hay sparse, burnt yellow as the oats. Both looked brittle. The villages, hard pressed to make even a thin living, were harsh and sunbaked, architectural echoes of the lined and weary peasants we saw in the fields. It was the countryside of so many French films and novels – hard, proud, suspicious and self-contained.

Perhaps the most extraordinary and persistent sight was the great nests of mistletoe in the trees that fringed the road.

We spent the night at the *Cloche* in Vitry le François, an excellent hotel as new as almost everything else in the town. Vitry is little more than one main *place*, a symmetrical square

surrounded by clean buildings which reproduce the France of
Louis XVI, from which roads run symmetrically from the
centre of each side. The cathedral alone, grey outside and
grimly unloved within, gave an air of antiquity. When we
asked the manager of the *Cloche* he gave us the answer we might
have expected.

'*C'était la guerre!*' The town was indeed as new as it looked.
Almost every building had been obliterated by the bombard-
ment.

I commented hesitantly on the little towns and villages of
Champagne, and the manager's face clouded.

'We are not a rich country, m'sieur. And the end of the war
is not much more than twenty years ago. You did not know
the meaning of being "occupied" in England. And when it was
all over those who "occupied" France got a great deal more
help in putting their country to rights than we did.'

It was not a subject to be pursued much further, and I
dropped it. France is an uneasy place for political discussions,
especially if one of the protagonists is British. Instead, I compli-
mented him, very properly, on his hotel. His frown was
dispelled.

'We are listed in the *Logis de France*, m'sieur.'

It was a fair comment. The *Logis de France* is worth knowing
about, especially for the motorist who keeps away from the
routes nationales and wants to avoid the bigger centres. It is an
organisation, voluntary and unallied to any major interest,
which lists hundreds of hotels, mostly outside the big towns,
where the tourist may be assured of a high standard of excel-
lence though not of opulence. The list is available from any
French Tourist Information Office and, in my opinion, is as
indispensable to the average traveller as the *Guide Michelin* to
the affluent.

Certainly we could not have been more comfortable than
at the *Cloche* in Vitry and *Le Chanzy* in Arras – both in the

Logis list. At dinner Paul chose *escargots* – but snails were not our own idea of high living, and he ate them alone. Typical of the hotel's open hospitality, the trim waitress brought a cheeseboard with seven varieties of cheese.

'All made near Vitry, ma'mselle,' she said to Susan. 'Try them all, and tell us which you like best.' It was an impossible task, and a difficult choice.

Here for the first time we really hit the tourist routes. The road from Paris to Strasbourg passes through Vitry's new square, and the still busier one from Paris and the north to Dijon, Marseilles and the Riviera. For the first time, too, we had four or five other GB cars parked by our own. In one, an elderly daughter was driving her spry, ninety-one-year-old mother to the Mediterranean. In another, a son was taking his parents in the same direction. The father had had a thrombosis and the mother was slowly recovering from a stroke.

The seven o'clock peal of the cathedral bells was, I hoped, entirely inappropriate. They rang across the square to the tune of *Nearer, my God, to Thee* – a curiously Protestant melody which I hoped the aged and the invalids did not recognise.

This, they said, is the land of the champagne vineyards – but not on *our* route. The only vineyard we passed on the way to Rheims next day was about twenty feet by thirty feet, on the piggery side of a farmyard. Nevertheless, Rheims proves the point, for it is the capital of the champagne industry.

It is also one of the oldest and most historic cities of France.

Its name derives from Remi, its patron saint who began the christianisation of France by baptising Clovis, king of the Francs, at this spot. So began the long tradition of royal coronations in Rheims. St Remi has his own splendid basilica, where his tomb and shrine are to be seen – but it is the magnificent cathedral that draws the visitor. It was filled with worshippers when we went in. And with visitors, too, most of them French, who made a gesture to piety by crossing themselves and then got busy sightseeing.

There are those who contend that Rheims is the greatest Gothic cathedral in the world, and many of its architectural treasures may support the claim. The arches, the great mediaeval 'sculpture gallery' on the west front, the magnificent rose window of this 13th-century shrine of Notre Dame are all superb. But, for me, it was enough to allow the contemporary worshippers to dissolve, in my mind, into the throng that crowded the cathedral in 1429. A girl in white armour dismounted from her charger outside the cathedral and led her ruler, the Dauphin, up to the altar to be crowned Charles VII of France. So Joan of Arc, shepherdess of Domremy and Maid of Orleans, came to Rheims in one of the most remarkable moments of French history. There must have been many who were more intrigued by the Maid than impressed by the king.

At the end of the First World War no more than a hundred houses remained in the lovely old town, and it is a high tribute to the city that it was rebuilt with such dignity and such sense of history. I shudder to think what might have happened today! Certainly they improved it, widening its streets and substituting good homes for insanitary old housing. Yet the essential magic of Rheims remains. The lovely *Place Royal*, for instance, with Louis XV on his charger in the centre, is as gracious as one could find anywhere in France.

But the last war gave it a still more remarkable monument. It was here, in the Technical College, that General Eisenhower had his headquarters, and the room with the bare table on which the Germans signed their capitulation remains as it was. With the operational maps still pinned to the walls, it is a bit of frozen history in a Europe that has changed beyond recognition.

We had hoped to see something of the town's greatest industry – champagne. To visit at any rate one of the big

companies and perhaps make our conducted way through some
of the eleven miles of underground cellars. But I cannot
describe what it is like, after all. In France, too, everything
closes at twelve! And noon had just struck.

Fifty kilometres beyond Rheims we glimpsed a curious and
apparently ruined citadel on the hill-top. Though no one else
seemed to be doing so, we left the *route nationale*, a mile from
the 'ruins', to go and investigate. Up a long, winding road we
came not to a ruin but to a town with modern streets. The
citadel turned out to be the *haute ville* of Laon, a town built like
many others – Bridgnorth, in Shropshire, for instance – both
on the hill and down below it. As usual, it was the old city,
fortified by towers and ramparts, which crowned the hill. We
spent an hour wandering round this enchanting old place.
The cathedral – or, rather, ex-cathedral, since its bishop was
moved to a city less tied to antiquity – was clean, fresh and
worshipful. Outside the streets were narrow and winding. The
episcopal palace, rising forbidding above them, had a notice
on the once-episcopal gate announcing a presentation of
mediaeval miracle plays – a sort of Coventry or York. The odd
thing was that none of the guide-books we turned up even
mentioned Laon as a town worth stopping for.

It certainly is, if only for its honesty. When we got back to
the square we found the boot of our car wide open. I must
have failed to catch it when I took out my camera. But, in
defiance of those unhappy tourists who have been robbed,
cheated and pilfered everywhere they went, not a thing was
touched or out of place.

Now the land was indeed flat. Its names were recent history.
St Quentin . . . Peronne . . . Bapaume . . . the battlefields of the
First World War . . . and, finally, Arras.

The town captivated us, and linked us with the beginning of
our journey. Here, like Bruges, were the tall Flemish houses,
with their stepped gables masking the steep roofs. Here was

the Town Hall with its Belfry, and the Grand' Place, cobbled and arcaded, all completely Flemish. The 17th-century air of both the great squares, with the hint of Spain that belongs to all Flemish public architecture, was almost undisturbed in the Sunday evening quietude. One of them, the bigger one, has a more violent atmosphere when it is given over to the town's private variety of ball-game, a sort of cross between St Columb's 'hurling' and American football. We wandered round the peaceful streets as darkness fell and could not believe we would sleep in England the following night. We ate well and slept well, and then set off for Boulogne and home.

There is really nothing more to report.

Back on English soil the sun was still shining as we came off the boat into Dover's busy streets and joined the long trek on the crowded road towards London. It had all been far easier than we dared to hope – and infinitely more rewarding. The roads had been better and less crowded than we had been told. So much quieter, indeed, even in France, that we decided to get away from this bumper-to-bumper queue. After all, we knew the Kent and Sussex roads from memory. We put the map away in the glove-box, turned off the main road, took a short cut for Reigate and home . . .

. . . And got lost !